MARXISM:
A RE-EXAMINATION

IRVING M. ZEITLIN
Indiana University

NEW PERSPECTIVES
IN
POLITICAL SCIENCE

Van Nostrand Reinhold Company

New York   Cincinnati   Toronto   London   Melbourne

To Esther

VAN NOSTRAND REINHOLD COMPANY Regional Offices:
Cincinnati New York Chicago Millbrae Dallas

VAN NOSTRAND REINHOLD COMPANY Foreign Offices:
London Toronto Melbourne

Copyright © 1967 by LITTON EDUCATIONAL PUBLISHING, INC.

Manufactured in the United States of America

Published by VAN NOSTRAND REINHOLD COMPANY
450 West 33rd Street, New York, N. Y. 10001

Published simultaneously in Canada by
D. VAN NOSTRAND COMPANY (Canada), Ltd.

8 7 6 5 4 3 2

Preface

KARL MARX THOUGHT OF HIMSELF AS A SCIENTIST AS WELL AS A revolutionary. He conceived of much of his work as providing both a scientific account of the nature of capitalism and a scientific basis for the socialist movement of his time. He advanced his general theory in order to guide the revolutionary action of the working class, the main agency through which the capitalist system was to be changed and ultimately superseded. The possibility of revolution rested on certain objective economic and political conditions which could be grasped through a careful study of the structure and tendencies of capitalism. In these terms, Marx's theory is empirically based and informed by the spirit of scientific inquiry. It is this aspect of Marx's social thought which is emphasized and made explicit in the present study.

I.M.Z.

Contents

I. The Philosophical Foundations of Marx's Social Thought

MARX'S RELATIONSHIP TO HEGEL

THE VIEW IS STILL PREVALENT THAT MARX'S THOUGHT IS ESSEN-tially Hegelian in its origin and character. Thus Robert C. Tucker, for example, asserts that "Marx founded Marxism in an outburst of Hegelizing." [1] According to the same view, Marx was a materialist and his accomplishments may therefore be summed up as having stood Hegel on his feet. Thus again we read in Tucker's work that Marx ". . . considered himself to be engaged in no more than a momentous act of translation of the already discovered truth about the world from the language of idealism into that of materialism." [2] This view, it will be argued, is inadequate for the following reasons: (a) it neglects Marx's opposition to Hegel which was actually more important in shaping Marx's ideas because it resulted in an original synthesis and not a mere translation of Hegelian truths into the language of materialism; (b) it conceals the fact that Marx's outlook cannot be adequately described as materialist; (c) it obscures the other important sources of Marx's thought; and finally, (d) it ignores the empirical basis of Marx's social theories. As Herbert Marcuse has observed, Marx's thought is in all respects a different order of truth as compared with Hegel's, and not to be interpreted in terms of the latter's philosophical concepts.[3] In order to grasp the extent to which this is true, it is necessary to challenge the prevailing view by re-examining Marx's relationship to his intellectual antecedents and contemporaries; and the most logical place to begin such a re-examination is with Hegel's philosophy.

1

HEGEL'S DIALECTICAL PHILOSOPHY

In Hegel the dialectical process has both conservative and radical implications, and works itself out in the following fashion. On the one hand there is at each phase of development the emphasis on slow, organic growth determined by immanent rational laws. Between phases, however, as in the transition from the acorn to the oak tree, there is a kind of "dialectical leap" from one quality (acorn) to another (oak tree), when the quantitative accumulation of slow organic change reaches a nodal point at which the addition of a quantum produces a qualitative change. This occurs through the process of the negation of the negation.[4] The acorn in this example was itself a negation of its previous form, the seed. With the continuation of the quantitative change, the acorn is also negated by the new and potential form within it—the oak tree. Contained already within the seed is the chain of opposing forces which, if the seed is to develop, must continue to negate one another until its full potential is actualized. Each thing contains its own negation and each is a unity of opposites. When a particular thing is "negated," it is superseded by a new form which continues to develop until it, too, engenders its own negation. This is precisely what "development" means—changing according to the immanent pattern of a given thing. Negation, then, is not synonymous with outright destruction, as by crushing the seed, for example. Negation occurs only when the initial form is transcended by new qualities inherent in it and when the new qualities in their subsequent development actualize the full potential of the initial form.

Things strive to attain *actually* what they always were *potentially* Hegel is saying in his own formulation of an essentially Aristotelian notion. In natural organisms, this takes place in a "direct, unopposed, unhindered manner. Between the Idea and its realization—the essential constitution of the original germ and the conformity to it of the existence derived from it—no disturbing influence can intrude." [5] In nature, typically, essence is actualized in existence as an undisturbed harmonious process. The opposite, however, is true in relation to Spirit, or the human, socio-cultural realm: "The realization of *its* Idea is mediated by consciousness and will. . . . Thus Spirit is at war with itself; it has to overcome itself as its most formidable obstacle. That development which in the sphere of Nature is a peaceful growth, is in that of Spirit, a severe, a mighty conflict with itself. What Spirit really strives for is the realization of its Ideal being; but in doing so, it hides that goal from its own vision, and is proud and well satisfied in this alienation from it." [6] Development in the socio-cultural sphere, therefore, ". . . does not present the harmless tranquility of mere growth, as does that of organic life, but a stern reluctant working against itself." [7] The dialectical development of the social realm is a process characterized by conflict. For in the cultural realm the development toward "freedom," far from being a natural and mindless process, is contingent upon consciousness and will. "Universal history . . . shows the development of the consciousness of Freedom on the part of the Spirit, and the consequent realization of that Freedom. This development implies a gradation—a series of increasingly adequate expressions or manifestations of Freedom, which result from its Idea. The logical, and—as still more prominent—the *dialectical* nature of the Idea in general, viz., that it is self-determined—that it assumes successive forms from which it successfully transcends; and by this very process of transcending its earlier stages, gains an affirmative, and, in fact, a richer and more concrete shape. . . ." [8]

Yet, this philosophy has its conspicuously conservative side. Much like Burke, Hegel argued that it is not the individual, nor even the family, but the State which is the embodiment of Law; the State is the highest order to which all others must subordinate themselves. Real World History begins with the State; and its Right and Law supersede all pre-historical forms with their right and law. "The State is the Idea of Spirit in the external manifestation of human Will and its Freedom. It is to the State, therefore, that change in the aspect of History indissolubly attaches itself. . . ." [9] And in the final analysis it is none other than the German Nation and the Prussian State which embody the true, the eternal wisdom of the Spirit. "We have now arrived," Hegel concludes, "at the third period of the German world, and thus enter upon the period of the Spirit conscious that it is free, inasmuch as it wills the True and Eternal—that which is in and for itself Universal." [10]

In effect, Hegel brought together in one philosophical synthesis the Enlightenment emphasis on reason and the Romantic conception of historical development as an organic process. Reason, he argued, is not merely a faculty existing in the individual by which he might measure and evaluate customs and institutions; it is inherent in the process of development itself. This is the meaning of the celebrated notion that "what is rational is real" and "what is real is rational." Reason is not, as the *Philosophes* had regarded it, a mere abstraction from the real, it is an immanent force which determines the structure and development of the entire universe. Thus when Hegel says that the rational is real, he means it as an ontological statement. In this way, Hegel transforms reason into a great cosmic force which he calls the Idea, the Spirit, the Absolute, or finally, God. This is not an unchanging essence but is continually developing and becoming. Moreover, it is an impersonal logical and cosmic process which unites the social as well as the natural realm; all customs, habits, institutions, and conceptions are united into one dynamic and organic whole. The historical process is the manifestation of the progressive unfolding of Reason in the various social and cultural institutions; and this development follows a form which is not essentially different from the way human thought develops. The cosmic reason develops and objectifies itself in institutions by the process of fusion of contradictions; this fusion produces new contradictions which in turn are brought together in a new synthesis, and so on to infinity. In other words, each thesis engenders its antithesis which are then both resolved into a synthesis which becomes a new thesis. If the cosmic reason is to be distinguished in any way from individual reason, it is by the more complete unfolding of the former's inherent potentialities. The individual mind can comprehend only aspects of reality. The acorn, however, becomes what it can become; it unfolds into an oak tree.

In the human realm, the nation stands higher than all other institutions for it is *the* vehicle through which the cosmic reason realizes its destiny. This becomes clear from Hegel's division of history into a series of succeeding epochs, each of which expresses a particular phase in the development of the World Spirit. When a nation is still in its ascending phase, it embodies not the whole of cosmic reason, but only a particular phase of its ultimate fulfillment. A nation is an individualized expression of the World Spirit and is therefore the medium through which the spirit achieves self-consciousness. For Hegel, this whole process culminated in the German Culture of his day, with the Spirit ultimately having reified itself in the Prussian State, the highest expression of the Cosmic Reason on earth. Hegel has brought the process to an arbitrary and abrupt stop—a surprising conclusion indeed.

One can see, then, two distinct and opposing tendencies in Hegel's thought. On the one hand, it led to the ideological defense of the Prussian State and of German society at the time, for many concluded that what is, is rational and therefore necessary and unavoidable. And besides, had not Hegel taught that this was the final and most perfect stage of history? In these terms, Hegel's philosophy became definitely conservative in its influence. But on the other hand, there was the emphasis on change, a dynamic and dialectical development which continues ceaselessly and inexorably.

The Left-Hegelians, a group including Friedrich Strauss, Ludwig Feuerbach, Bruno Bauer, Moses Hess, and Marx and Engels, drew some logical conclusions from the radical tendency in Hegel's philosophy and adopted a stance very similar to that of the Enlightenment thinkers a century before: They criticized mercilessly everything irrational in the existing social order, for in this way the boundaries of freedom would be widened. But whereas the other members of the group continued to limit their activity to criticism of the church, its dogma, and other institutions and ideas, Marx soon concluded that this was not enough. In Marx's view, these young Hegelians were now hardly to be distinguished from the old; they were staunch conservatives who never realized that they could not change the existing world merely by combating the phrases of this world. Marx thus began to develop his own theory of society and history which led him eventually to demand a total transformation of society. This theory will be examined in detail later; meanwhile, we want to determine the sense in which Marx employed a dialectical method and how it compared with that of Hegel.

MARX'S DIALECTICAL CONCEPTION OF SOCIETY AND HISTORY

Although Marx, as a young man, was a close student of Hegel and was educated in an atmosphere dominated by the latter's philosophy, he did not remain a disciple of Hegel. The position taken here is that Marx developed his social and political theories in opposition to Hegel's philosophy and that the latter was little more than an "erstwhile philosophical conscience" with which Marx settled accounts early in his life.

Marx rejected all the metaphysical premises of Hegel's philosophy including his mystical conception of the dialectic. In the Afterword to the second German edition of the first volume of *Capital,* Marx dissociated himself from Hegel's idealism, and spoke of his own method in contrast to Hegel's:

> My dialectical method is not only different from the Hegelian, but its direct opposite. To Hegel, the life-process of the human brain, i.e., the process of thinking, which, under the name of "the Idea," he even transforms into an independent subject, is the demiurgos of the real world, and the real world is only the external, phenomenal form of "the Idea." With me, on the contrary, the ideal is nothing else than the material world reflected by the human mind, and translated into forms of thought.[11]

Much earlier both Marx and Engels had dissociated themselves from the "Old" and Young Hegelians alike. In *German Ideology,* which they completed by the summer of 1846, they wrote:

> The Old Hegelians had *comprehended* everything as soon as it was reduced to an Hegelian logical category. The Young Hegelians *criticized* everything by attributing to it religious conceptions or by pronouncing it a theological matter. The Young Hegelians are in agreement with the Old Hegelians in their belief in the rule of religion, of concepts, of an abstract general principle in the existing world. . . .
>
> The young Hegelian ideologists, in spite of their allegedly "world-shattering" statements, are the staunchest conservatives. . . . They forget . . . that they are in no way combating the real existing world when they are merely combating the phrases of this world . . . .
>
> It has not occurred to any of these philosophers to inquire into the connection of German Philosophy with German reality, the relation of their criticism to their own *material* surroundings.[12]

As early as 1846, then, Marx and Engels had emphasized their so-called *materialist* standpoint in contrast to Hegelian idealism.

In fact, already in his manuscripts of 1844, Marx had devoted a whole section to a critique of Hegel in this spirit and had praised Ludwig Feuerbach for basing his philosophy on the relation of man to man.[13] Marx had begun to develop his own conception of history in these manuscripts. Though he himself never used the term "dialectical materialism,"[14] he did speak of his dialectical method, as we have seen, and it is important to understand in what sense he employed such a method.

In the manuscripts of 1844, Marx's moral outlook and ethical commitment took the form of secular-humanism; and this remained the impulse behind his life's work. Marx saw as the secular function of man the process of self-emancipation which was to be accomplished by *self-activity,* by man's action upon nature and upon other men. At the center of this process was the labor activity of living men engaged in the process of production. However, neither man's daily productive activity nor his efforts toward self-emancipation were a peaceful, tranquil, and harmonious process. Marx had been alerted by Hegel's concepts of negation and contradiction to the conflictive character of the social realm. But Marx employed these concepts in a series of hypotheses and propositions which guided his empirical studies of the capitalist system. The various terms of the Hegelian dialectic are thus basically transformed; for if Marx sees "contradictions" in the existing social system, these are not imputed to the system in an *a priori* fashion. On the contrary, his method of inquiry is inductive and his conclusions are presented, illustrated, and sometimes even dramatized by means of dialectical terminology. That this was Marx's intention is clear:

> Of course the method of presentation must differ in form from that of inquiry. The latter has to appropriate the material in detail, to analyze its different forms of development, to trace out their inner connection. Only after this work is done, can the actual movement be adequately described. If this is done successfully, if the life of the subject-matter is ideally reflected as in a mirror, then it may appear as if we had before us a mere a priori construction.[15]

At the same time, Marx wants to salvage the useful rational kernel in Hegel's dialectic. Marx writes:

> In its rational form, [the dialectic] is a scandal and abomination to bourgeoisdom and its doctrinaire professors, because it includes

in its comprehension and affirmative recognition of the existing state of things, at the same time also, the recognition of the negation of that state, of its inevitable breaking up; because it regards every historically developed social form as in fluid movement, and therefore takes into account its transient nature not less than its momentary existence; because it lets nothing impose upon it, and is in its essence critical and revolutionary.[16]

Essentially, then, what Marx took from Hegel was his emphasis on reason and on negative, critical thinking; and he integrated this way of thinking into his intellectual consciousness. With Marx, however, this aspect of dialectical thinking was not only critical, but empirical and scientific as well. Conflict is explained in terms of concrete and specific social relationships. One class owns the means of production while the other does not; this is the basis of the various forms of conflict between them. Marx views the entire capitalist system as resting on conflicting tendencies: "contradictions" exist between the social character of production and the institution of private property; between the "productive forces" and the existing "relations of production"; between production and consumption; between private landownership and rational agriculture, and so on. All of these conclusions are arrived at inductively. For Marx, the negative aspects of reality are rooted in definite social conditions; and his dialectical reasoning is therefore quite the opposite of Hegel's closed ontological system. Does this then mean that it would be correct to characterize Marx's view as materialistic? This must be answered in the negative. For while Marx opposed Hegel and rejected idealism in general, he developed his own dialectical view by rejecting equally the materialism prevalent in his time.

Marx took a firm position against the way of thinking which claimed that the basis of all mental and spiritual phenomena was to be found in matter and material processes. This kind of materialism—promulgated in Marx's time by one Karl Vogt—taught that emotions and ideas are sufficiently explained as results of chemical bodily processes. One of Vogt's most popular phrases was "Ideas stand in the same relation to the brain as bile does to the liver or urine to the kidneys." [17] Marx rejected this way of thinking as mechanical, "bourgeois" materialism which ignored human history and the social activity of real men. So repugnant to him was this doctrine—certainly not less so than idealism—that he postulated instead what he called in the *Economic and Philosophic Manuscripts* ". . . naturalism or humanism [which] is distinguished from both idealism and materialism, and at the same time constitutes their unifying truth." [18] Thus the problem of settling accounts with his philosophical past was for Marx a complicated matter. Although he rejected the idealism of Hegel, and for that matter all idealism in the ontological sense, he saw in it a rational kernel which had to be salvaged; and while he rejected the prevailing form of materialism, he saw in it an important truth which had to be disclosed by eliminating its defects. This is best brought out in Marx's first thesis on Feuerbach.

> The chief defect of all hitherto existing materialism—that of Feuerbach included—is that the thing [*Gegenstand*], reality, sensuousness, is conceived only in the form of the *object* [*Object*] or of contemplation [*Änschauung*], but not as *human sensuous activity, practice,* not subjectively. Hence it happened that the *active* side, in contradistinction to materialism, was developed by idealism—but only abstractly, since, of course, idealism does not know real, sensuous activity as such. Feuerbach wants sensuous objects, really differentiated from the thought objects, but he does not conceive *human activity* itself as *objective* [*Gegenstandliche*] activity.[19]

Even earlier, in his doctoral dissertation, Marx revealed his dissatisfaction with the passivity inherent in mechanistic materialism and his admiration for the "active side" which idealism grasped and developed. His dissertation dealt with the differences between Democritean and Epicurean natural philosophy.[20] Democritus was regarded as the father of materialism, for he, more than any other of the older natural philosophers of Greece, adhered most closely to materialism.[21] Out of nothing only nothing can come. All that exists cannot be destroyed. Change is nothing but the coming together and pulling apart of particles of matter. Everything happens with reason and necessity and not fortuitously. Existence is nothing but atoms and space; the atoms are infinite in number and in the variety of their forms. The larger atoms, falling eternally through infinite space, collide with the smaller atoms, and the moving matter which results is the beginning of the formation of worlds. These worlds form and pass away, coexistently and successively.

Epicurus accepted this conception from Democritus but introduced certain changes, the most important of which, and most subject to ridicule from Cicero to Kant, was the so-called "swerve of the atoms." [22] They did not fall vertically but in a deviation from the straight line. Unlike Democritus who concerned himself only with the material existence of the atom, Epicurus went further and treated the atom as a conception. For Epicurus the atom was not only the material basis of the world of phenomena, but also the symbol of the individual and his self-consciousness. Thus while Democritus's view led him to conclude the necessity of all occurrences, Epicurus, causing his atoms to swerve from the straight line, made room for free will, the will of the living human being wrested from the inexorability of his fate. It is for this reason that Marx passed an unfavorable verdict on Democritus and a favorable one on Epicurus. What turned Marx against Democritus was the absence of an "energizing principle," or as he later put it in his theses on Feuerbach: The chief weakness of all previous materialism was the comprehension of the thing, reality, sensualism only in the form of object and not subjectively as practical, human activity. Epicurus, on the other hand, had seen the subjective, active side, and Marx admired him for this. Marx's conclusions will no doubt come as a surprise to anyone who has attributed to him a crass materialism. Marx was as far from mechanistic materialism as he was from idealism, and neither term adequately describes his outlook. His philosophy is neither idealism nor materialism but a synthesis of humanism and naturalism. Marx developed his synthetic view in critical opposition to Hegel as early as his *Economic and Philosophic Manuscripts of 1844* [23] and not later than his *German Ideology* and *Theses on Feuerbach* completed in 1846. Any impression to the contrary may be due to the Hegelian style which he employed throughout his life, even in his late writings. But he is explicit on this score. He was merely flirting with Hegel's *style* in his later works because he resented his former master being treated as a "dead dog." In 1873 Marx wrote:

> The mystifying side of Hegelian dialectic I criticized nearly thirty years ago, at a time when it was still the fashion. But just as I was working at the first volume of "Das Kapital," it was the good pleasure of the peevish, arrogant, mediocre *epigoni* who now talk large in cultured Germany to treat Hegel . . . as a "dead dog." I therefore openly avowed myself the pupil of that mighty thinker, and even here and there, . . . coquetted with the modes of expression peculiar to him.[24]

Marx wanted to pay his respects but could do so only by turning his former master on his feet. This interpretation of Marx's relation to Hegel as having turned the latter right side up, should be given its proper emphasis. The main point for Marx was not that he was a materialist and Hegel an idealist in the epistemological sense. That much was true. More important was the fact that Hegel, Feuerbach, *and* the mechanical materialists, had missed the essentially *creative role of human activity and conduct.* Hegel's grasp of this fact was unsatisfactory because it was strictly metaphysical. In Marx's view, Hegel understood the importance of the labor process but only in an alienated form, as the movement of pure disembodied spirit.

> The outstanding achievement of Hegel's Phenomenology . . . is, first, that Hegel grasps the self creation of man as a process . . . and that he therefore grasps the nature of *labor,* and conceives objective man (true, because real man) as the result of his *own* labor.[25]

Hegel conceived of history as a movement and conflict of abstract principles which controlled real individuals. Political and economic categories, which he nevertheless understood and described very well, were projected into the heaven of pure thought, and the philosopher became witness, judge, and redeemer of the alienated world. For Marx this conception had to be turned right side up. This he attempted by emphasizing that history is the activity of real men and that this activity can be studied objectively by beginning with the social conditions under which men live and not primarily with their ideas. Marx developed this conception in opposition to Hegel and was therefore far from being his disciple. If the contrary impression persists, that Marx was primarily indebted to Hegel for his own approach to history, then it is probably a result not only of Marx's flirtation with the Hegelian style but also of certain superficially analogous features common to both of them.

For example, it has been argued that Hegel viewed historic development as the struggle of opposites and that Marx derived his conception of history from the former, retaining the notion that history was "logical in its development . . . advancing by contradiction, and the negation of the negation." [26] Max Eastman and others have thus interpreted Marx's conception of class conflict as a variation on Hegel's dialectical theme. According to this view

Marx was therefore indebted to Hegel for one of his central social theories which thus becomes an *a priori* construction rather than an inductive proposition based on empirical-historical evidence. However, this resemblance is insufficient evidence for asserting that such was the origin of Marx's theory of class struggle, particularly since Marx explicitly acknowledged another source. In that acknowledgment Marx wrote:

> . . . no credit is due to me for discovering the existence of classes in modern society, nor yet the struggle between them. Long before me bourgeois historians had described the historical development of this struggle of the classes and bourgeois economists the economic anatomy of the classes.[27]

Marx therefore owed his conception of the historical character of classes and the struggles between them not to Hegel but to certain French historians, particularly Guizot and Thierry; and he was led to the study of the economic anatomy of classes by the English economists, particularly Adam Smith and Ricardo.

In considering Marx's relationship to Hegel, there is still another idea which, though Hegelian in origin, was fundamentally transformed in the hands of Marx. *Alienation,* for Hegel, like his other constructs, was exclusively a phenomenon of the mind. With the Young Hegelians the concept was significantly altered but remained primarily a philosophical notion, viz., a condition in which man's own powers appear as independent forces or entities controlling his actions. Feuerbach, for instance, used the concept of alienation in his explanation of religious phenomena and viewed extramundane beings as man's own invention. Describing Feuerbach's view, Engels wrote: "Nothing exists outside nature and man, and the higher beings our religious fantasies have created are only the fantastic reflection of our own essence." [28] Marx began where Feuerbach left off. The problem of alienation is no longer a philosophical problem for Marx. He treats it as an explicitly social phenomenon. Going beyond Hegel and Feuerbach, Marx asked, "In what circumstances do men project their own powers, their own values, upon hypothetical, superhuman beings: What are the social causes of this phenomenon?" [29] Alienation for Marx was a condition in which an object produced by the hands of man "stands opposed to [him] as an *alien being,* as a *power independent* of the producer." [30] Men feel alienated because work has ceased to give them a sense of purpose and the mastery over nature for which they strive. The worker ". . . does not fulfill himself in his work but denies himself, has a feeling of misery rather than well-being, does not develop freely his mental and physical energies, but is physically exhausted and mentally debased." [31] For Marx, whether it is commodity-fetishism or idolatry, alienation expresses itself in the worship of something into which man has placed his creative powers and to which he now submits. Indeed, the striking parallel between idolatry of Old Testament times and the various fetishisms of material goods in our day provides a clearer idea of what Marx meant by alienation. Theologians[32] have pointed to idolatry as a manifestation of alienation while psychologists have probed the phenomenon in the following terms:

> The essence of what the prophets call "idolatry" is not that man worships many gods instead of only one. It is that the idols are the work of man's own hands—they are things, and man bows down and worships things . . . . He transfers to the things of his creation the attributes of his own life, and instead of experiencing himself as the creating person, he is in touch with himself only by the worship of the idol.[33]

Just as the idol becomes a power over man by obscuring the real source of his strength and creativity, so, under capitalism, the commodities and the instruments of production which man himself creates are seen as possessing powers over him. But this is the same sort of illusion as seeing a creative force in an idol. To shatter this illusion and disclose the power behind the instruments of production became one of Marx's central objectives in his analysis of the capitalist system.[34]

We have seen that Marx's intellectual orientations are a complicated matter and not to be understood as an adaptation of the Hegelian dialectic. Moreover, Marx never spoke of the dialectic in nature but rather limited its application to the socio-historical realm. Engels, however, seems to have regarded the dialectic differently.

In some cases he uses the concept simply to designate the mutability of all being; in others, he invokes at least two parts of the "triadic principle," speaking of (a) *quantitative* change culminating in a new *quality,* and (b) the mode of change of reality proceeding by *negation of the negation.* In addition, Engels seems never to have decided whether the dialectic was an ontology or heuristic device.[35] He constantly emphasized that one must proceed empirically and inductively in studying all phenomena. After careful study, however, he believed that one will discover what he thought science was revealing each day anew: the dialectical character of natural and social phenomena.

In his introduction to *Dialectics of Nature,* written in 1875-76, Engels stressed the mutable character of nature. Nature does not just exist, but *comes into being and goes out of being.* Not only the earth as a whole but also its surface and the plants and animals living on it possess a history in time.[36] Later in the same introduction he wrote of a mode of contemplation which he considered superior to the metaphysical. Again he seems to equate this mode of contemplation simply with viewing all being as in a constant state of flux. It was his view that "all nature, from the smallest thing to the biggest, from grains of sand to suns, from protista to man, has its existence in eternal coming into being and going out of being, in ceaseless flux, in unresting motion and change." [37] Thus Engels presented a point of view which he called dialectical and with which few would quarrel today.

Later, in 1877, in *Socialism: Utopian and Scientific,* he continued to employ the same definition but made clearer what he meant by contrasting the dialectical with the so-called metaphysical view.

> When we consider and reflect upon nature at large or the history of mankind or our own intellectual activity, at first we see the picture of an endless entanglement of relations and reactions, permutations and combinations, in which nothing remains what, where and as it was, but everything moves, changes, comes into being and passes away.[38]

Engels regarded this view bequeathed to us by the ancient Greek philosophers, particularly Heraclitus, as a correct one and adequate to comprehend the "picture as a whole." But it did not suffice, in his opinion, "to explain the details of which this picture is made up, and so long as we do not understand these, we have not a clear idea of the whole picture." [39] To grasp these details, Engels believed, was the task of both the natural and the social sciences. The sciences, however, in their method of isolating parts of a whole in order to comprehend them had left us

. . . as legacy the habit of observing natural objects and processes in isolation, apart from their connection with the vast whole; of observing them in repose, not in motion; as constants, not as essentially variables; in their death, not in their life.[40]

In addition to constant change, then, Engels considered the interdependence and interconnection of phenomena a fundamental postulate of the dialectical method. And if this were all he attributed to the method, i.e., comprehending the changeful and interdependent aspects of reality, almost no one would object to his assertion that nature is the proof of dialectics. However, Engels did attribute more to the method and, indeed, to nature itself.

In 1894, Engels wrote in his preface to *Anti-Duhring* that his studies of mathematics and natural science were undertaken to convince himself of what in general he was not in doubt, namely, ". . . that in nature, amid the welter of innumerable changes, the same dialectical laws of motion force their way through as those which in history govern the apparent fortuitousness of events . . . ."[41] In the quotation above he attributes "dialectical laws of motion" to nature. A few pages later, while underscoring the role of natural science in comprehending the dialectical character of nature, he adds that this can be done more easily with an "understanding of the laws of dialectical *thought*."[42] Up to this point, despite the ambiguity of his formulation, if all that Engels meant is that everything changes and everything is interdependent in varying degrees, and that this should always be kept in mind, it is probably an acceptable view, especially if understood heuristically. But Engels complicated matters by adding the concept of *contradiction*.

In his chapter on *quantity* and *quality* he argued that

Motion itself is a contradiction; even simple mechanical change of position can only come about through a body being at one and the same moment of time both in one place and in another place, being in one and the same place and also not in it. And the continuous origination and simultaneous solution of this contradiction is precisely what motion is.[43]

This formulation imputes the "contradiction" to motion itself, which is quite different from saying that the concept of contradiction may be fruitful for the comprehension of motion as a phenomenon. Engels never clarified which meaning he assigned to the dialectic; that is, whether he viewed it as a method separate and distinct from the general scientific one. He went on to argue that even life itself is a contradiction.

Later, in his chapter on the negation of the negation, Engels attempted to defend one of Marx's statements in *Capital*. There Marx discussed the expropriation of the smaller producers by the larger in the process of concentration and centralization of capital. Marx's statement appears thus:

> The capitalist mode of appropriation, the result of the capitalist mode of production, produces capitalist private property. This is the first negation of individual private property, as founded on the labor of the proprietor. But capitalist production begets, with the inexorability of a law of nature, its own negation. It is the negation of negation.[44]

Here it will be well to remember that it was passages such as these that Marx had in mind when he said that he coquetted with the Hegelian style. In the quoted statement, then, the content must be separated from the form. That capitalism begets its own negation with the "inexorability of a law of nature" is an empirical statement for Marx, arrived at after a careful study of capitalism as an economic and social system, and Marx is employing Hegelian terms to dramatize his conclusions.

How did Engels view this formulation? First he agreed that by ". . . characterizing the process as the negation of the negation, Marx [did] not intend to *prove* that the process was historically necessary." [45] (Italics mine.) In continuing, however, Engels introduces a notion which appears to be at odds with Marx's intention. "Only after he [Marx] has proved from history that in fact the process has partially already occurred, and partially must occur in the future, he in addition characterizes it as a process which develops in accordance with a definite dialectical law." [46] Clearly this is open to at least two interpretations. Either Marx's empirical method was sufficient to reveal the character of capitalist production, and the dialectical vocabulary was employed merely to dramatize his conclusions; or the capitalist mode of production develops in accordance with a definite dialectical law which may be grasped independently of any empirical method. The latter is suggested in Engels' concluding statement that "the law of the negation of the negation . . . is unconsciously operative in nature and history . . . ." [47] Which interpretation Engels intended we shall never know. Because he never clarified the issue for himself, the dialectic became in the hands of his followers precisely what he wanted to avoid: an *a priori* lever for the construction of history. And this consequence was certainly at odds with Marx's view of the dialectic.

In summary, it may be true that if Marx is to be taken seriously as a philosopher, his Hegelian origins must be given due weight.[48] But it is at least equally important to give his opposition to Hegel due weight. To understand Marx's social theories, other intellectual origins besides Hegel have therefore to be considered.

MARX AND SAINT-SIMON

The influence of Saint-Simonian ideas upon Marx is unmistakable. Many of Saint-Simon's disciples were active in Germany, but the best known among those who had any direct association with Marx was Moses Hess. Hess was a close student of French "Utopian" socialism. Indeed, "Paris was Hess's second home in the eighteen-forties, when the ideas of Saint-Simon . . . were discussed in pamphlets and journals, argued on street corners, and preached from the lecture platform." [49] It was Hess, quite a few years older than Marx and Engels, who, in 1842, recommended Marx to the editorial board of the *Rheinische Zeitung* and who first suggested that he take socialism seriously and acquaint himself with the works of the French socialists.[50] Apparently Hess tried to synthesize the views of Spinoza and Saint-Simon and introduced the Young Hegelians to French sociology.[51] This took place precisely at the time when Marx and Engels had not only critically opposed Hegel but had seen the defects in Feuerbach's philosophy as well. Where Feuerbach fell back, Hess rushed in to fill the breach.

> He blamed the Hegelian philosophy of history for refusing the task of deducing the future from the past and the present and of proceeding to influence its formation. This is a typical Saint-Simonian idea, and later it was to become a corner-stone in the system of Marx and Engels.[52]

Moreover, Marx may have been exposed to Saint-Simon's ideas even before he began to study Hegel's philosophy.[53] While he was still in high school in Trier, Saint-Simon's disciples had become so active and numerous in the region that the archbishop issued a warning against their "heresy." One of them, Ludwig Gall, who published a Saint-Simonian pamphlet in 1835, belonged to the same literary society as Marx's father and the headmaster of his school. Another Saint-Simonian, Eduard Gans, delivered lectures at the University of Berlin, among the first that Marx attended when he had begun his studies there in 1837. Evidence that this exposure had a primary and profound influence on Marx appears in the very Saint-Simonian emphasis he placed on industry and labor. To demonstrate this similarity, a few of Saint-Simon's propositions will be examined and compared to those of Marx.

For Saint-Simon, the reorganization of European societies was a major objective which could only be accomplished on the basis of science and industry. They were to be the twin bases of the new society and were to exercise hegemony over mankind. This view as well as his conception of the developing industrial system and its impact on the feudal order clearly influenced Marx.

> Since the emancipation of the towns [Saint-Simon wrote] we have seen the industrial class, after it had purchased its freedom, succeed in making itself a political force. . . . It is growing and enriching itself gradually, and is becoming more important. Its social condition is being improved in every way, while the classes which may be termed theological and feudal continued to lose in prestige and real power. Hence I conclude that the industrial class is bound to continue its progress and finally to dominate the whole community.
>
> This is an inevitable development and the old institutions, which already have lost the power to maintain what they originally built up, will fall forever and disappear of their own accord.[54]

The growth of the new system—increasingly incompatible with the older one—is seen by Saint-Simon as the cause of the French Revolution.

> This tremendous crisis [the French Revolution] did not at all have its origin in this or that isolated fact. . . . It operated as an overturning of the political system for the simple reason that the state of society to which the ancient order corresponded had totally changed in nature. A civil and moral revolution which had gradually developed for more than six centuries engendered and necessitated a political revolution . . . .[55]

Marx not only accepted this explanation of the decline of feudalism, he applied its logic to the capitalist order as well. If the growth of the bourgeoisie had served to undermine the feudal system, then the growth of a class-conscious proletariat would have the same consequences for capitalism.

What eventually led Marx to a critique of Saint-Simon's doctrine was the fact that the latter regarded as the productive class all those who actively participated in industrial society—whether they were owners or not. This lumping together in one class of owners and non-owners was, in Marx's view, Saint-Simon's fundamental error. He had not understood that the third estate was not of a piece and that its victory over the older classes was "the victory of a small part of this 'estate,' . . . the propertied bourgeoisie." [56] Engels nevertheless acknowledged his genius. "Already in his Geneva letters, Saint-Simon lays down the proposition that 'all men ought to work.' " He recognized the reign of terror as the "reign of the non-possessing masses." He interpreted the French Revolution as a class war, and, Engels observes, ". . . to recognize the French Revolution as a class war . . . between nobility, bourgeoisie, and the non-possessors, was, in the year 1802, a most pregnant discovery." [57] Finally, Saint-Simon, like Marx after him, viewed politics as the "science" of production. Saint-Simon

. . . foretells the complete absorption of politics by economics. The knowledge that economic conditions are the basis of political institutions appears here only in embryo. Yet what is here already very plainly expressed is the idea of the future conversion of political rule over men into an administration of things and a direction of processes of production—that is to say, the "abolition of the state" . . . . [58]

Here, Engels may have been acknowledging Saint-Simon as the source for Marx's ideas about the "withering away of the state."

So much for Saint-Simonian ideas which definitely must be taken into account when considering the various sources of Marx's social thought. But there is still another intellectual tradition which must be looked at in this regard.

THE ENGLISH CLASSICAL ECONOMISTS

The English classical economists also had a major influence upon Marx. As early as his *Economic and Philosophic Manuscripts of 1844,* Marx showed an intimate knowledge of Adam Smith's *Wealth of Nations* which is extensively quoted in the manuscripts. [59]

At that time, he had also read at least sporadically in Ricardo and James Mill.[60] The range of other English economists who influenced Marx's thinking later in life may be gathered from the copious documentation of sources conveniently provided in the Index of Authorities, an appendix to the first volume of *Capital*. Marx's erudition in English economics was vast and he was profoundly influenced by this body of thought. This is what prompted Joseph Schumpeter to remark that

> As an economic theorist Marx was first of all a very learned man . . . [Nothing] in Marx's economics can be accounted for by any want of scholarship of training in the technique of theoretical analysis. He was a voracious reader and an indefatigable worker. *He missed very few contributions of significance.*[61] (Italics mine.)

This erudition was acquired in his mature years, in the course of his prolonged stay in Victorian England. One tends sometimes to forget that Marx arrived in London in 1849 and made his home there until his death in 1883. During that time though he devoted himself to political agitation, propagandistic activities and the like, his main energy was spent working on his chief work, *Das Kapital*, which in some respects can be read as a continuation of the work begun by the English economists who preceded him.

Marx's life in England became one of scholarship—he spent long hours each day in the library of the British Museum in London, and almost all of the data and empirical materials which he employed in his research were drawn from English authors and English experiences. To support his hypotheses and general propositions, he used the current statistics and other information from the financial column of the *Economist*, and from the Blue Books—reports compiled by the factory inspectors for the Royal Commissions of Inquiry.

Throughout *Capital*, he develops his theoretical view on the basis of the work of Smith, Ricardo, and others. He uses some of their main assumptions and theories, e.g., the labor theory of value; but here too as in the case of the other intellectual traditions on which he draws, he adds to these theories, modifies them, and finally transforms them so that the product takes on a fundamentally new meaning.

To take an example of his indebtedness to this tradition, the main outlines of what he called the anatomy of classes, and the relationship of the economic to the other institutional orders of society, were to be found at least implicitly in the writings of the English economists. To be sure, Adam Smith, for example, did tend to separate his economic *Inquiry into the Nature and Causes of the Wealth of Nations* from the other general questions of law and government, just as he gave separate attention to the problem of moral sentiments. Nonetheless, he addressed himself in his economic work not only to fundamental economic relations, but also to the new political and social conditions which arose from the development of industry, exchange of commodities, and the division of labor within the new socio-economic system. The same is true of Ricardo who also keeps before him the interdependence of political economy with the rest of the social order. Marx, of course, eventually goes beyond these thinkers to formulate an original theory—his materialist conception of history—but remains indebted to them for basic insights.

And if Marx was critical *and* scientific in *Capital,* this was not the first example of such an approach. His critical dialogue with his predecessors was not an innovation. Long before him ". . . the mercantile system had been criticized by the Physiocrats, the Physiocrats by Adam Smith, and Adam Smith by Ricardo." [62] The last of these, brilliant though he was, had not transcended the bourgeois standpoint, for he had treated "the antagonism of class interests, of wages and profits, of profits and rent" as if they were the results of an inexorable law of nature, and hence destined to remain always with mankind.[63] Yet, as Marx acknowledged, Ricardo did point before him to the inherent conflict of interests existing among the classes of industrial society. In the preface to his *Principles of Political Economy and Taxation,* Ricardo states that the main purpose of this science is to determine how the "produce of the earth—all that is derived from its surface by the united application of labour, machinery, and capital—is divided among three classes of the community; namely, the proprietor of the land, the owner of the stock or capital necessary for its cultivation, and the labourers by whose industry it is cultivated." Marx retained this three-class model in *Capital.*[64]

Also, while Ricardo had in his earlier work assumed that the "general good" is something of an inevitable outcome of the economic system of his time, he eventually revised that opinion and concluded that "the opinion entertained by the labouring class, that the employment of machinery is frequently detrimental to their interests, is not founded on prejudice and error, but is conformable to the correct principles of political economy." [65] Thus while he retained an over-all view of the system which was positive, he was also objective and in some respects critical of the consequences of what Marx was later to call capitalism. Even Ricardo's principles—principles not uniquely his—were assailed for encouraging class conflict. Marx relates that a contemporary of his, an American economist called C. H. Carey, attacked Ricardo ". . . as a man whose works are an arsenal for anarchists, Socialists, and all the enemies of the bourgeois order of society. He reproaches not only him but Malthus, Mill, Say, Torrens, Wakefield, McCulloch, Senior, Whately, R. Jones, and others, the masterminds among the economists of Europe, with rending society asunder and preparing civil war because they show that the economic bases of the different classes are bound to give rise to a necessary and ever-growing antagonism among them." [66]

In Marx's view, the high degree of objectivity of classical economics in England was limited to the period in which the conflict between workers and capitalists was as yet undeveloped. Ricardo was the last great representative of that tradition, for after him the class-struggle became more intense, in France as well as England, and ". . . took on more and more outspoken and threatening forms. It sounded the knell of scientific bourgeois economy. It was thenceforth no longer a question whether this theorem or that was true, but whether it was useful to capital or harmful, expedient or inexpedient, politically dangerous or not. In place of disinterested inquirers, there were hired prize-fighters; in place of genuine scientific research, the bad conscience and the evil intent of apologetic." [67] Marx thus decried what he regarded as the increasingly ideological character of postclassical political economy.

There is no doubt that Marx took the classical tradition quite seriously, and that his own theory was to a significant degree shaped by that tradition.

MARX'S ETHICAL OUTLOOK

Marx's moral commitment and ethical outlook, which were in fact the motive force of his life's work, may be seen as a synthesis of naturalism and humanism, or in a word, secular-humanism. This philosophical outlook caused him to focus early in his life on the process of man's self-activity, his action upon nature and other men.

The assumption is still widespread, particularly among those with only a superficial acquaintance with Marx's writings, that he attached no importance to the individual. According to this assumption, Marx's ideal was to feed and clothe every man, woman and child, without a comparable interest in their spiritual or psychological needs. Marx is held to deny all spiritual values and this seems ". . . all the more apparent to those who assume that belief in God is the condition for a spiritual orientation." [68]

In his recent study of Marx's manuscripts of 1844, Erich Fromm declares this popular picture of Marx's "materialism" as utterly false.

> Marx's aim was the spiritual emancipation of man, of his liberation from the chains of economic determinism, of restituting him in his human wholeness, of enabling him to find unity and harmony with his fellow man and with nature. Marx's philosophy was, in secular, non-theistic language, a new and radical step forward in the tradition of prophetic messianism; it was aimed at the full realization of individualism, the very aim which has guided Western thinking from the Renaissance and the Reformation far into the nineteenth century.[69]

To many this will no doubt sound like an overdrawn picture, completely at odds with the impression they hold of Marx's outlook. In part this is understandable since until recently no explicit philosophical statement by Marx was available in English. Although Marx's humanism is implicit in all of his writings, the most explicit statement of his ethical outlook is found in the recently translated *Economic and Philosophic Manuscripts of 1844* cited above. This, his main philosophical work which he wrote as a young man, deals with the concepts of alienation and man's self-activity toward the goal of emancipation. The fact that these manuscripts have not been available to the English-speaking world is not sufficient, however, to explain the prevailing false impression of Marx's world view. Fromm has aptly observed that

> . . . the fact that this work of Marx's had never before been translated into English is in itself as much a symptom as a cause of the ignorance; . . . because the main trend of Marx's philosophical thought is sufficiently clear in those writings previously published in English to have avoided the falsification which occurred.[70]

Of course, there are additional reasons for the misunderstanding of Marx's outlook. The various acts and policies carried out in the name of Marxism have certainly added their share to the misunderstanding and antipathy for Marx and his work.

The main point to be made here is that Marx was moved in *all* his work by humanist values and had as his ideal the kind of society in which material interest would cease to be the dominant one. This ideal, in turn, moved him to focus attention on the worldly activity of men, the main and most essential form of this activity being productive physical and mental labor. Given the continual development of the "material" basis, or the productivity of men, and the superabundance which Marx envisioned as a result of it, man could, by abolishing all relations of servitude, leave the domain of "necessity" and enter the domain of freedom. This view, most consistently expressed in his manuscripts and other early writings, is one he did not desert in his maturity. For example, in *Capital* he wrote:

> The life-process of society, which is based on the process of material production, does not strip off its mystical veil until it is treated as production by freely associated men, and is consciously regulated by them in accordance with a settled plan. This, however, demands for society a certain material groundwork or set of conditions of existence which in their turn are the spontaneous product of a long and painful process of development.[71]

As a young man Marx stated similar ideas in more philosophical terms:

> . . . the emancipation of society from private property, from servitude, takes the political form of the *emancipation of the workers;* not in the sense that only the latter's emancipation is involved, but because this emancipation includes the *emancipation of humanity as a whole.* For all human servitude is involved in the relation

of the worker to production, and all types of servitude are only modifications or consequences of this relation.[72]

It will be recalled from our discussion of alienation that this concept was central to Marx's interest. The phenomenon in its general form, to which he was alerted by Hegel and afterwards by Feuerbach and which he reinterpreted in more precise social terms, occupied the center of his attention as a young man. But it recurs, as we shall see, throughout his later writings in such concepts as "commodity fetishism," and the general accumulation of capital over which man increasingly loses control. It was alienation which Marx saw as the manifestation of man's loss of freedom, that condition under which "the object produced by labor, its product, now stands opposed to it as an alien being, a power independent of the producer." [73] The aim of eliminating this condition underlay his entire life's work. Socialism and/or communism were therefore not ends in themselves, but means of abolishing human self-alienation.

> Communism is the positive abolition of *private property,* of *human self-alienation,* and thus the real *appropriation of human nature* through and for man. It is, therefore, the return of man himself as a *social,* i.e., really human, being, a complete and conscious return which assimilates all the wealth of previous development. Communism as a fully-developed naturalism is humanism and a fully-developed humanism is naturalism. It is the *definitive* resolution of the antagonism between man and nature, and between man and man. It is the true solution of the conflict between existence and essence, between objectification and self-affirmation, between freedom and necessity. . . .[74]

The "leap" from necessity to freedom—the overcoming of alienation and the achieving of emancipation—was possible only by means of man's self-activity, labor and industry. Marx brought these categories down to the solid ground of economic and social analysis and attributed a creative role to labor. Through labor man makes himself and eventually provides the basis for his freedom.

Thus, in part as a negative reaction to Hegel's exclusive concern with the spiritual realm and in part as a positive insight which he gained from Saint-Simon and the English economists, Marx came to stress the role of labor as basic in the *creation of men,* in the changes wrought in the forms of their social organization, and in bringing about the society of the future. The expression, "the role of labor in the creation of man," is appropriate because it is evident from the work of Marx and Engels that this was precisely the importance which they assigned to labor. Labor, they believed, was the fundamental factor even in the creation of man—or more correctly in the differentiation of men from their closest zoological relatives.

In a short, speculative essay entitled *The Part Played by Labor in the Transition from Ape to Man*, Engels attempted to deal with this problem. In this essay the role Marx and Engels assigned to labor may be clearly seen. Labor was the basis of the developing interaction and cooperation among the proto-hominids. It provided the basis for rudimentary social organization and for the changes in this organization which culminated in human society and the creation of man.

"Labor," wrote Engels, "is the prime basic condition for all human existence, and this to such an extent that, in a sense, we have to say that labor created man himself." [75] When man's simian ancestors were compelled, for whatever reason, to descend to the ground and make it their predominant habitat, the use of their organs changed in adapting to their new mode of life. They learned to walk without the aid of their hands and to adopt a more and more erect gait. The hand was freed from its crutch-like function and this was "the decisive step in the transition from ape to man." [76] For the erect gait to have become first the rule and then a necessity "presupposes that in the meantime diverse other functions increasingly devolved upon the hands." [77] At first these hand operations were simple. But the most ancient and primitive of these man-like creatures had achieved something of which their closest zoological relatives were incapable. "No simian hand ever fashioned even the crudest of stone knives." [78] With time, hand operations became increasingly complex and the hand acquired even greater dexterity and skill. These skills were passed on from generation to generation.

"Thus the hand is not only the organ of labor, *it is also the product of labor*." [79] But the hand did not develop in isolation. "It was only one member of an entire, highly complex organism. And what benefited the hand, benefited also the whole body. . . ." [80]

These gregarious creatures in transition were struggling to master their new habitat. It was this struggle which created social man. In Engels' words:

> The mastery over nature, which began with the development of the hand, with labor, widened man's horizon at every new advance. He was continually discovering new, hitherto unknown, properties of natural objects. On the other hand, the development of labor necessarily helped to bring the members of society closer together by multiplying cases of mutual support, joint activity, and by making clear the advantage of this joint activity to each individual.[81]

Cooperation provided the need for oral communication and was simultaneously facilitated by it.

> First labor, after it and then with it speech—these were the two most essential stimuli under the influence of which the brain of the ape gradually changed into that of man, which for all its similarities is far larger and more perfect. Hand in hand with the development of the brain went the development of its most immediate instruments—the sense organs.[82]

Thus man's various senses and faculties ". . . developed only side by side with the development of the human hand itself, through the medium of labor." [83]

Concomitantly with the development and interaction of the various activities of these early men, labor, speech, the brain and the senses made for "increasing clarity of consciousness, power of abstraction and of judgment." [84] The latter in turn imparted to labor and speech an ever-renewed impulse to further development.

Men learned to consume everything edible and to live in every climate. Their labor became diversified, and the various tasks were divided among them. These tasks ultimately included mental as well as physical ones. And the more the activity of these men assumed the character of premeditated, planned action directed toward definite ends known in advance, the further removed they became from their animal relatives. This, in brief, is how Marx and Engels viewed the process of how man made himself.

To summarize, it has been argued that for a clearer understanding of Marx's social thought, more attention should be given to his divergence from Hegel than to his Hegelian origins. The attempt was made to substantiate the proposition that, already as a young man, Marx developed a thoroughgoing criticism of Hegel and his dialectic. Marx's method was inductive and empirical, his occasional employment of Hegelian vocabulary notwithstanding. Marx learned much from Hegel, Saint-Simon and the English classical economists; he selected certain elements of their thought and rejected others so that the result was an original synthesis.

Finally, it was shown that Marx was a secular-humanist morally committed to changing the human condition. He sought the explanation of all social phenomena within the complex relationship of society to nature without any extra-mundane residue. This view, for which he was groping in his manuscripts, eventually became a mature conception of the development of man and of human society. This conception will gain in clarity with the further exploration of Marx's work.

NOTES

1. Robert C. Tucker, *Philosophy and Myth in Karl Marx.* Cambridge: Cambridge University Press, 1961, p. 123.

2. *Ibid.,* p. 123.

3. Herbert Marcuse, *Reason and Revolution.* Boston: Beacon Press, 1960, p. 258.

4. See Hegel, *Science of Logic,* translated by W. H. Johnston and L. G. Struthers. New York: The Macmillan Company, 1951, Vol. I, p. 147 ff.

5. G. W. F. Hegel, *The Philosophy of History.* New York: Dover Publications, Inc., 1956, p. 55.

6. *Ibid.,* p. 55.

7. *Ibid.,* p. 55.

8. *Ibid.,* p. 63.

9. *Ibid.,* p. 47.

10. *Ibid.,* p. 412.

11. Karl Marx, *Capital,* Vol. I. Moscow: Foreign Languages Publishing House, 1954, p. 19.

12. Karl Marx and Frederick Engels, *The German Ideology.* New York: International Publishers, 1960, pp. 5-6.

13. Karl Marx, *Economic and Philosophic Manuscripts of 1844.* Moscow: Foreign Languages Publishing House, 1961, pp. 142-171.

14. This term was apparently coined by Plekhanov as was "historical materialism" by Engels. See T. B. Bottomore and Maximilien Rubel, *Karl Marx: Selected Writings in Sociology and Social Philosophy.* London: Watts and Co., 1961, p. 20.

15. *Capital* Vol. I. Moscow: Foreign Languages Publishing House, 1954, p. 19.

16. *Ibid.,* p. 20.

17. Franz Mehring, *Karl Marx*. Ann Arbor: The University of Michigan Press, 1962, p. 280.

18. Karl Marx, *Economic and Philosophic Manuscripts,* translated by T. B. Bottomore in Fromm, *Marx's Concept of Man.* New York: Frederick Ungar Publishing Co., 1961, p. 181. These manuscripts are hereafter cited as E.P.M.

19. Karl Marx, *Theses on Feuerbach* in Karl Marx and Frederick Engels, *Selected Works* Vol. II. Moscow: Foreign Languages Publishing House, 1951, p. 365. The *Selected Works* are hereafter cited as MESW.

20. The following remarks are based on the discussion of Marx's doctoral dissertation in Franz Mehring, *op. cit.,* pp. 25-31, and in H. P. Adams, *Karl Marx in His Earlier Writings.* London: George Allen & Unwin Ltd., 1940, pp. 27-41.

21. Bertrand Russell, *A History of Western Philosophy.* New York: Simon & Schuster, 1963, pp. 64-72.

22. *Ibid.,* p. 246.

23. An entire section of these manuscripts is devoted to a criticism of Hegel and is in fact called: "Critique of the Hegelian Dialectic and General Philosophy." In this section Marx takes the Young Hegelians to task for remaining within the confines of Hegelian logic. See Karl Marx, E.P.M., pp. 142-171, or Moscow edition, pp. 169-196.

24. Karl Marx, *Capital* Vol. I, pp. 19-20.

25. Marx, E.P.M., p. 177.

26. Max Eastman, *Marxism: Is It Science?* New York: W. W. Norton & Co., Inc., 1940, p. 73.

27. Marx in a letter to J. Weydemeyer, March 5, 1852; MESW II, p. 410.

28. Engels, *Ludwig Feuerbach and the End of Classical German Philosophy,* MESW II, pp. 332-333.

29. Bottomore and Rubel, *op. cit.,* p. 4.

30. Marx, E.P.M., p. 95.

31. *Ibid.,* p. 98.

32. See, for example, Paul Tillich, *Der Mensch im Christentum und im Marxismus,* Dusseldorf, 1953, and Jean-Yves Calvez, *La Pensee de Karl Marx.* Paris: Editions Du Seuil, 1956.

33. Fromm, *op. cit.,* p. 44.

34. In moving toward this objective it seems that Marx and Engels abandoned the term "alienation" in favor of more precise scientific terms. This becomes evident particularly in their writings of the late 1840's where they began to use the concepts of "struggle" and "exploitation." In the course of their intellectual development they groped for a more scientific and politically more effective terminology. This does not mean, however, that the *problem* of alienation did not dominate all their writings. It appears again and again in their mature work and is variously described as "commodity-fetishism," the ac-

cumulation of capital and its consequences for the worker, the separation of the worker from the means of production, etc. The popularity of this concept today is itself an interesting question. Lewis Feuer has suggested that it suits the present conditions of prosperity and indicates the shelving of any mood for basic economic reconstruction. Under conditions of prosperity, critics of the social order have focused on the psychological aspects of the superstructure and not on the economic basis. For a provocative discussion of the problem see Lewis Feuer, "What Is Alienation? The Career of a Concept," in *Sociology on Trial*. Edited by Maurice Stein and Arthur Vidich. Englewood Cliffs: Prentice-Hall, Inc., 1963, pp. 127-146.

35. In this discussion the following points should be kept in mind: (a) Both Marx and Engels believed that "true consciousness" was a relatively adequate reflection of "reality." They were never bothered by problems of mediated knowledge and gave no attention to the theory of knowledge which emphasizes the role of the intervening *a priori* categories in shaping perception, learning, etc. For Marx and Engels, *being* and *thinking* were a unity and they therefore would have deemed it objectionable to employ a dualism such as the noumenal and phenomenal. Conceivably it is for this reason that Engels did not carefully distinguish between the dialectic as a useful method, and the allegedly dialectical character of nature and society. (b) The differences between the two thinkers in their approach to the dialectic may very well have been a function of their intellectual division of labor. It was Engels who took upon himself the task of clarifying their approach to the natural sciences. This, together with the polemical character of his writing, may have led to an approach which is here criticized for its vagueness and is expressed in his vacillation between positivism and Hegelianism. (c) Of course, our critique of Engels should not be construed as a denial of the heuristic value of dialectical thinking.

36. Engels, Introduction to *Dialectics of Nature,* MESW II, p. 63.

37. *Ibid.,* p. 65.

38. Frederick Engels, *Anti-Duhring*. Moscow: Foreign Languages Publishing House, 1954, p. 33.

39. *Ibid.,* p. 33.

40. *Ibid.,* p. 33.

41. *Ibid.,* p. 17.

42. *Ibid.,* p. 22.

43. *Ibid.,* p. 167.

44. *Ibid.,* p. 186.

45. *Ibid.,* p. 186.

46. *Ibid.,* p. 186.

47. *Ibid.,* p. 197.

48. George Lichtheim, "Marx and His Critics," *Problems of Communism,* Vol. XI, No. 4, July-Aug. 1962, pp. 43-46.

49. John Weiss, *Moses Hess Utopian Socialist.* Detroit: Wayne State University Press, 1960, p. 3.

50. *Ibid.,* p. 10.

51. See Gustav Mayer's discussion of this point in *Friedrich Engels.* New York: Alfred A. Knopf, 1936, p. 26.

52. *Ibid.,* p. 27.

53. Some evidence on this point is presented in E. M. Butler, *The Saint-Simonian Religion in Germany,* Cambridge, 1926, and in B. Nicolaievsky and O. Maenchen-Helfen, *Karl Marx Man and Fighter.* Philadelphia and London: J. B. Lippincott Co., 1936. In addition, Bottomore and Rubel cite Kovalevsky as recalling in his reminiscences that Marx spoke of his father-in-law, Ludwig von Westphalen, as an enthusiastic disciple of Saint-Simon. See Bottomore and Rubel, *op. cit.,* p. 9.

54. *Henri Comte De Saint-Simon, Selected Writings.* Edited and translated by F. M. H. Markham, Oxford: Basil Blackwell, 1952, p. 70.

55. *Oeuvres Complètes de Saint-Simon et Enfantin,* Paris, 1865-76, *Du Système Industriel,* V, p. 77.

56. Engels, *op. cit.,* p. 356.

57. *Ibid.,* p. 358.

58. *Ibid.,* p. 358.

59. See particularly the chapters on "Wages of Labor and Capital" in *Karl Marx,* E.P.M., Moscow Edition, *op. cit.,* pp. 20-51.

60. *Ibid.,* p. 95.

61. Joseph A. Schumpeter, *Capitalism, Socialism and Democracy.* New York: Harper and Row Publishers, Inc., 1962, p. 21.

62. Karl Korsch, *Karl Marx.* New York: Russell and Russell, 1963, p. 101.

63. Karl Marx, *Capital* Vol. I. Moscow: Foreign Languages Publishing House, 1954, p. 14.

64. This is true particularly in the later volumes. In Vol. I, as we shall see, he uses a two-class model—a result of his method of abstraction. This will be discussed in Part Two.

65. *Principles of Political Economy,* Chapter XXXI.

66. *Marx and Engels: Selected Correspondence.* Moscow: Foreign Languages Publishing House, 1953, p. 85.

67. *Capital,* Vol. I. Moscow: Foreign Languages Publishing House, 1954, p. 15.

68. Fromm, *op. cit.,* p. 2.

69. *Ibid.,* p. 3.

70. *Ibid.,* p. 6.

71. Marx, *Capital* Vol. I, p. 80.

72. Marx, E.P.M., p. 107.

73. *Ibid.,* p. 95.

74. *Ibid.,* p. 127.

75. Frederick Engels, *The Part Played by Labor in the Transition*

from Ape to Man, MESW II, pp. 74-85. This discussion should not be construed as an endorsement of Engels' exposition, or of its scientific accuracy from the standpoint of modern anthropology. It is presented here only for the insight it may provide into the conception Marx and Engels held of the labor process and its role in the creation of human society.

76. *Ibid.,* p. 74.
77. *Ibid.,* p. 75.
78. *Ibid.,* p. 75.
79. *Ibid.,* p. 75.
80. *Ibid.,* p. 76.
81. *Ibid.,* p. 76.
82. *Ibid.,* p. 77.
83. *Ibid.,* p. 77.
84. *Ibid.,* p. 78.

II. Marx's Conception of the Capitalist Mode of Production

MARX'S MODEL

THE FUNDAMENTAL HUMAN ACTIVITY, AS VIEWED BY MARX, WAS the *labor process;* he wished to employ the concept for a scientific understanding of the structure of society and the processes by which it changed. In this sense, his interests went far beyond the economic spheres of human activity, and even beyond political economy. This becomes clear not only from the wide variety of social phenomena which he studied, but especially from a plan for a large-scale study of societies in general, and of capitalist society in particular.

In his *Grundrisse der Kritik der Politischen Ökonomie,* which he began in 1857, Marx outlined the following themes which he had planned to investigate in detail.

1. The abstract characteristics common to all forms of society, taking into account their historical aspects.

2. The main constituent elements of the internal structure of bourgeois society, upon which the basic social classes rest, capital, wage labour, and landed property. Town and country. The three great social classes. The exchange between them. Circulation. Credit.

3. Crystallization of bourgeois society in the form of the state. The "unproductive" classes. Taxation. Public debt. Public credit. Population. Colonies. Emigration.

4. International relations of production. International exchange. Exports and imports. Exchange.

5. The world market and crises.[1]

Marx never carried out this plan in its entirety. The parts which he did complete, however, make this much clear: He was not a methodological realist, i.e., he attributed no reality to society apart from the individuals comprising it. He wrote, "It is above all necessary to avoid postulating 'society' . . . as an abstraction confronting the individual. The individual *is* a social being." [2] Society for Marx refers to individuals in their interrelations or interaction. He considered the most important sphere of social interaction the sphere of material production, or the labor process. This process expressed the relationship of men to nature, and to one another; as the former relationship changed, so did the latter. "Marx's earliest and dominating interest was in historical change . . . . His intention, at least, was to give a scientific account of social change. . . ." [3] In order to grasp Marx's conception of the capitalist system, an understanding of its mode of production is necessary. Only by considering this mode of production in detail is it possible to uncover the process of change as Marx saw it.

In *Capital,* Marx employed an abstract-deductive method which was also characteristic of the Ricardian school.[4] More specifically he practiced what has been called the method of "successive approximations," which consists in moving from the more abstract to the more concrete. In this method, simplifying assumptions are removed at successive stages of the investigation so that "theory may take account of and explain an ever wider range of actual phenomena." [5] Clearly, the fruitfulness of this method depends on the ability of the investigator to separate the essential from the nonessential. What did Marx consider to be the essential?

His interest was society as a whole and especially the process of social change. The economic structure and within it the sphere of production was the most significant for Marx because it is here, he believed, that the main impetus to social change is to be found. His aim was to discover and to explain the relationship between this sphere and all other spheres of social action. Once having concluded that the key to social change is to be found in the mode of production, he was effectively committed to study it carefully and exhaustively. For Marx the most essential relationship in the capitalist mode of production was that between the capitalists and the workers. These two classes created by the capitalist system also determined the operation of the system. Therefore the basic relationship between them had to form the center of his investigation and abstraction was necessary to isolate the relationship and reduce it to its purest form. In this way he could subject it to painstaking analysis undisturbed by unrelated influences. In developing this method, Marx compared himself to a physicist. "The Physicist either observes physical phenomena where they occur in their most typical form and most free from disturbing influence, or, wherever possible, he makes experiments under conditions that assure the occurrence of the phenomenon in its normality." [6] To approximate these conditions in the study of society, Marx had to do the following. First, he had temporarily to think away all social relations except that between capital and labor.[7] Second, he had to choose the most *significant* form of this relationship. Significance for Marx was not a quantitative question. Paul Sweezy has explained this rather well: "It does not mean that the most frequent, or modal, forms of the relation must be selected for analysis. Significance, in this context, is a question of the structural characteristics and tendencies of the whole society. Marx, as is well known, selected the forms of capital-labor relation which arise in the sphere of industrial production as the most significant for modern capitalist society. Capitalists and workers are alike reduced to certain standard types, from which all characteristics irrelevant to the relation under examination are removed." [8] In *Capital,* Marx dealt with individuals only in so far as they personified economic categories, i.e., as embodiments of particular class relations and class interests. The entire first volume of *Capital* is at this high level of abstraction.

Thus Marx's method consisted in the construction of a *model,* a model constructed on the basis of the capitalist system on its classic ground, in England. There he could study the capitalist mode of production—the mechanics of the system—in its purest form. "That is the reason why England is used as the chief illustration in the development of my ideas." [9] To the extent, then, that he attributed "laws" of development to capitalism—or in more contemporary terminology, trends or tendencies—these were as he saw them in the classic home of capitalism. These trends were included in his model not in order to generalize them to every capitalist system, but, on the contrary, to confront the systems in other countries and empirically determine the extent to which the model fit. He no doubt attributed certain tendencies to all capitalist systems. But as we shall see in a later discussion, he considers in each case how the general conditions and trends are modified by the historically specific circumstances of each country. Keeping Marx's method of abstraction in mind, our discussion of the capitalist system can begin.

THE ORIGINS OF THE CAPITALIST SYSTEM

Money and commodities antedate the capitalist system. These are no more capital than means of production or means of subsistence. For Marx "commodity" has a very specific meaning and is something more than a mere product of labor. A "product" has only use-value and the producer typically produces it for his own consumption. A commodity also has use-value; otherwise there would be no point in producing it. Unlike the fruit of man's labor which is merely a product, the commodity has exchange-value, and is produced primarily for that purpose, i.e., to be exchanged. Typically, the exchange of commodities is facilitated by money. For Marx a commodity is congealed labor time, the objectification of labor; it is precisely this quality which makes commodities commensurable while at the same time creating the illusion that it is money that renders them so. "It is not money that renders commodities commensurable. Just the contrary. It is because all commodities, as values, are realized human labor, and therefore commensurable, that their values can be measured by one and the same special commodity, and the latter be converted into the common measure of their values, i.e., into money." [10]

Money and commodities are not yet capital for Marx. They were transformed into capital under certain very specific circumstances. This required that ". . . two very different kinds of commodity-possessors . . . come face to face and into contact; on the one hand, the owners of money, means of production, means of subsistence, who are eager to increase the sum of values they possess, by buying other people's labor power; on the other hand, free laborers, the sellers of their own labor-power, and therefore the sellers of labor." [11] These laborers are free in a double sense; they are neither a part of the means of production, as in the case of slaves and bondsmen, nor are they owners of means of production as in the case of peasant proprietors. In the absence of these conditions, or kinds of freedom, capitalism could never have arisen. The origin of the system, then, rests on the social process which separates the worker from his means of subsistence and production, while these means come under the exclusive control of the capitalist. Marx called this process the primitive accumulation of capital which makes its appearance within the framework of the feudal system.

The first industrial capitalists had to be free from the control of the feudal lords and the guilds. The workers, on the other hand, also had to be free from the various forms of feudal servitude and the regime of the guilds. Large masses of men were "suddenly and forcibly torn from their means of subsistence, and hurled as free and 'unattached' proletarians on the labor market." [12] Marx acknowledged the various forms which this expropriation took in different countries and in different periods. He described the process in England where he believed it had its classic form.

By the end of the 14th century serfdom was almost nonexistent in England. The majority of the population consisted of free peasant proprietors and agricultural wage-laborers. Both enjoyed usufruct of the common lands. A century later the feudal lords had so little an economic function, and as a consequence so little power, that it was relatively easy for the monarchy to break up the feudal retainers. A mass of free proletarians was hurled on the labor market. The great feudal lords, on their part ". . . created an incomparably larger proletariat by the forcible driving of the peasantry from the land . . . and by the usurpation of the common lands." [13] These forceful evictions had an economic basis. The Flemish wool manufacturers were prospering and this led in turn to a rise in the price of wool in England. Marx described the new nobility as the child of its time for which "money was the power of all powers. Transformation of arable land into sheep walks was, therefore, its cry." [14] He explores the process of expropriation from the 16th to the 18th century until it becomes clear how the two main classes of capitalist society emerged. Some of the evicted became vagabonds, sturdy yeomen roaming the countryside. The rest, a great mass, became available as proletarians, with nothing to sell but their labor-power, to the entrepreneurs awaiting them.

These were the origins of the two main classes of Marx's model, the two classes whose relationship becomes the basis of the capitalist system. All other classes and strata were temporarily ignored by him for the sake of the model. His focus on what he regarded as the two major classes of the capitalist system does not mean that he considered the action of "older" and intermediary classes as inconsequential for the actual system. Marx preferred the two-class model because it facilitated the analysis of the tendencies of the system in its "pure" state. It will be seen later, in the discussion of Marx's theory, that in his analysis of actual political and economic events he took all classes and strata into his purview.

THE TWO MAIN CLASSES OF THE CAPITALIST SYSTEM

The Buying and Selling of Labor Power

Marx explored the relationship of the two classes on the basis of the reciprocity expressed in the buying and selling of labor-power; a reciprocity, however, which is for Marx asymmetrical. While in legal terms both buyer and seller meet in the market place with equal rights, closer scrutiny reveals a relationship of dependence of the seller on the buyer. The origin of the seller was a condition of servitude and with his forcible eviction from the land he now enters a new condition of servitude. He owns no means of subsistence or production and has nothing to sell but his labor-power.

For Marx the term *labor-power* has a specific meaning and must be distinguished from *labor*. *Labor-power* refers to the capacity for labor, "the aggregate of those mental and physical capabilities existing in a human being, which he exercises whenever he produces a use-value of any description." [15] *Labor,* on the other hand, refers to the actual commodities produced by the worker while expending his labor-power. The worker sells not the commodities in which his labor is congealed but the commodity which is labor-power itself, and which exists only in his living self. This distinction enabled Marx to discover the basis of capital accumulation and the "exploitative" character of the capitalist system.

This was one of the discoveries which Engels attributed to Marx and which he designated as one of Marx's major contributions to social thought, namely, the *theory of surplus-value*.[16] For Marx the "secret" of capital accumulation lay in the unique character of the commodity which the worker offered for sale, labor-power. In Marx's words, the use-value of this commodity ". . . possesses the peculiar property of being a source of value, whose actual consumption . . . is itself an embodiment of labor, and, consequently, a creation of value." [17] The value of any commodity is determined by the labor-time *socially necessary* for its production. Likewise with the commodity called labor-power. Its value is determined by the labor time socially necessary for its production. Marx explained his conception of labor-power quite succinctly:

> Labor-power exists only as a capacity, or power of the living individual . . . . Given the individual, the production of labor-power consists in his reproduction of himself or his maintenance. For his maintenance he requires a given quantity of the means of subsistence. Therefore the labor-time requisite for the production of labor-power reduces itself to that necessary for the production of those means of subsistence; in other words, the value of labor-power is the value of the means of subsistence necessary for the maintenance of the laborer.[18]

Means of subsistence should not be confused with means of existence. It certainly includes the latter. The laborer must be maintained from one day to another and this requires the fulfillment of the needs for his survival. But subsistence is more than food, shelter, and the like. It is the product of historical development and will vary according to time and place depending on the customary degree of comfort in which the class of workers has been formed.

The labor-power consumed by wear and tear, age and death must be continually replaced. This means that the worker's subsistence must include the means necessary to support those who will replace him, i.e., his children. Otherwise, this class of peculiar commodity-owners could not perpetuate itself as a class and guarantee its appearance in the market.

Now the capitalist, on his part, has to be in a position to purchase labor-power and pay its value. He must have the wherewithal to pay not only for the labor-power but for the means of production necessary to produce, for only then can he utilize the labor-power and thereby gain value greater than his investment. This presupposes a class in an advantageous position, i.e., owners of the means of production. The two classes meet and exchange their respective commodities. But the purchaser of a commodity has a right to its use; he owns it. Therefore, from the instant that the worker enters the shop, the use-value of his labor-power, i.e., all that he produces, belongs to the capitalist. It is at this point that Marx thought he had made an important discovery. He believed that he had solved a problem over which many economists before him had cudgeled their brains and he called his solution the surplus-value theory.

Marx attempted to indicate the socio-historical bases of the owners and non-owners under capitalism. He argued that it was the historically determined advantageous position of the capitalist which enabled him to purchase labor-power. On the other hand, it was the historically determined subordinate position of the workers which separated them from their means of production and subsistence and rendered them dependent upon the capitalist for survival. Once the system came into being it was by appropriating surplus-value, i.e., by exploiting the worker, that the capitalist could increase his wealth and power, and at the same time perpetuate the dependence of the worker.

The theory of surplus-value is important because it attempts to explain the origin of the "surplus-quantity" which appears in every society when its economic development has reached a certain stage but which fulfills a special function under capitalism. For Marx the important point here was that under capitalism, in contrast to all previous systems, the surplus is invested in the expansion of the productive apparatus. The latter, as part of the developing "productive forces" of the system, became for Marx the "dynamic principle" of the capitalist system.

The theory rests on the assumption that the value of labor-power and the value of the product created by the worker during the production process are two different quantities. The difference is what the capitalist appropriates and typically invests in the expansion of capital. The expansion of capital, a central tendency under capitalism, allows for the growth of the "productive forces" within the system and eventually determines the changes in the other institutional orders of society. A brief illustration of the theory is in order here. It is based on Chapter VI of *Capital*. For convenience I use a set of arbitrary figures.

The Surplus Value Theory

For the sake of simplicity it is assumed that we are dealing with only one capitalist and one worker. The capitalist is interested in production not for its own sake but for a profit. He owns the means of production which includes the machines and the raw material—in this case cotton—which is to be transformed in the process of production. He needs a worker to operate the machine and thereby produce yarn which becomes the property of the capitalist and which he will offer for sale in the market. It is further assumed that the length of the working day in England at the time is 12 hours, and that the capitalist has a large store of cotton at his disposal in addition to the sum of money required to employ a worker.

The capitalist makes available to the worker the cotton and the machine. The price of the cotton is $5.00 for 10 pounds. He knows from experience that in the process of transforming 10 pounds of cotton into an equal amount of yarn, his machine will depreciate to the extent of $1.00. He agrees to pay his hired worker the prevailing daily wage, $1.50, which in turn is the value of the worker's labor-power. The worker begins his task and continues it for 6 hours, at the end of which the capitalist interrupts the process. Of course, the interruption occurs only in the illustration. He interrupts the process to see how matters stand, to take stock of his financial affairs.

He reflects on the fact that his man has been at work for 6 hours and that during that time 10 pounds of cotton have indeed been transformed into 10 pounds of yarn. The raw material cost him $5.00; the depreciation of the machine—or more correctly the value transferred by the machine to the product—cost him $1.00; the wages he paid the worker cost him $1.50. He adds it all up and finds that his total cost, which is at the same time the value of the yarn, equals $7.50. If he were to go to market with his yarn at this point—assuming he could dispose of it all at its value, i.e., 75 cents per pound—he could realize only what it cost him, $7.50, and not a penny more. Our capitalist is astounded; he cannot realize a profit on the sale of his yarn. Marx dramatizes the capitalist's consternation in the following imaginary soliloquy:

Can the laborer merely with his arms and legs, produce commodities out of nothing? Did I not supply him with the materials, by means of which, and in which alone, his labor could be embodied? And as the greater part of society consists of such ne'er-do-wells, have I not rendered society incalculable service by my instruments of production, my cotton and my spindle, and not only society, but the laborer also, whom in addition I have provided with the necessaries of life?[19]

To this Marx replies ". . . but has not the laborer rendered the equivalent service of changing his cotton and spindle into yarn?" [20]

And here Marx proceeds to explain the "secret" of the whole matter. The capitalist remembers that he has more than 10 pounds of cotton on hand; he knows too that the spindle has many more hours of life within it. Moreover, what is most important, he remembers that the worker has given him only 6 hours. But did he not pay the worker a full day's wage, $1.50, so that he could work a full day, 12 hours, and even subsist beyond that until the following morning? The capitalist is sorry he interrupted the process. He decides to resume it. He brings to the worker the additional raw cotton, sets him down at the spindle, and puts him to work for the balance of the day. At the end of the day the worker has worked not 6 but 12 hours, and has transformed not 10 but 20 pounds of cotton into an equivalent quantity of yarn. What is more, he has used the spindle 6 more hours.

Once more the capitalist sits down to assess the situation. Now instead of $5.00 the raw cotton cost him $10.00; the depreciation of the spindle cost him not $1.00 but $2.00. What about the additional labor time? If he paid the worker another $1.50, he would be right back where he started from. And this is precisely the point. He need not pay the worker another $1.50. The original $1.50 was a full day's wage, i.e., payment for 12 hours. Had he indeed stopped the process after the first 6 hours he never could have realized a profit. As matters now stand, however, the worker has given him the use of his labor-power for a full 12 hours and has produced in that time 20 pounds of yarn. The capitalist has received the product of his man's labor. The worker has received payment not for his labor but for his labor-power, i.e., his subsistence.

Adding up his cost once more the capitalist finds that the 20 pounds of raw cotton cost him $10.00; the depreciation of the machine $2.00; and the labor-power $1.50. He now proceeds to the market to sell his yarn again at the prevailing price, 75 cents per pound. Assuming that he succeeds in disposing of all 20 pounds, he is able to realize $15.00, or $1.50 more than it cost him. The sum over and above the cost of the worker's subsistence can now be pocketed by the capitalist; it is surplus-value. Marx further clarifies this process in these terms: "If we now compare the two processes of producing value and of creating surplus-value, we see that the latter is nothing but the continuation of the former beyond a definite point." [21]

Of course, this process may be clear neither to the capitalist nor to the worker. What Marx believed is very clear under feudalism, for example, is cloaked in mystery under capitalism. The serf knew very well what part of the day he worked for himself, and what part for the lord. The worker under capitalism, on the other hand, is not aware of the process by which he turns everything but subsistence over to the capitalist.

The theory of surplus-value indicates the sources of revenue of the classes under capitalism; and it accounts for the change and development of the capitalist system through the expansion of capital made possible by the appropriation and reinvestment of the surplus-value. The significance of the theory may best be seen in the function Marx understood the surplus-product to perform in the capitalist system.

In every society, with the possible exception of the primitive horde, there appears some sort of surplus product over and above the subsistence requirements of the producers themselves. In all such societies a group other than the producers was able to usurp the surplus product and, gaining control of it, use it toward its own ends. This became the economic basis of social stratification in these societies. The feudal system provides a striking example of this phenomenon.

Whatever the origin of the system, i.e., whether we accept the "force" theory of its origin or any other, it is clear that the perpetuation of the superordinate position of the various ranks of lord rested on the yield of agricultural production in the hands of the serfs. The latter worked part of the time for themselves and the remainder of the time for the lord. In terms of the legal theory of the feudal "contract" the relationship between the lord and serf was based on reciprocity; in actuality, however, it was based on the subordination of the serf by means of varying degrees of legitimized force. Both the legal and the power structures would have come toppling to the ground—Marx would argue—were it not for the capability of the serfs to produce a surplus-product in excess of their subsistence needs as these had come to be defined historically. Under feudalism the lords typically consumed the surplus-product without an eye to the expansion of production. Under capitalism, in contrast, the capitalists allocate a substantial part of the surplus-product for the expansion of the means of production. Marx contrasted the two systems in these terms: "Conservation of the old modes of production in unaltered form, was . . . the first condition of existence for all earlier industrial classes. Constant revolutionizing of production . . . distinguishes the bourgeois epoch from all earlier ones." [22] Under capitalism the largest portion of the surplus-value is invested in the expansion of the means of production. Marx described this central tendency in various ways which will be explored in the next section. Before proceeding to it, however, a short discussion of what Marx meant by the "organic composition of capital" is in order.

Marx made a distinction between *constant* and *variable*[23] capital which is quite different from and not to be confused with the conventional distinction between fixed and circulating capital. Constant capital refers to the outlay for machines and raw material, while variable capital refers only to wages, i.e., outlays for labor-power. The relation of constant to variable capital Marx calls the *organic composition of capital*. The greater the ratio of constant to variable, the higher the composition. Conversely, the greater the ratio of the variable portion, the lower the composition. The importance of this concept lies in the tendency under capitalism and perhaps in all societies for the constant to grow relative to the variable part, the latter growing only in absolute terms. This phenomenon was variously described by Marx as the general law of capital accumulation, the rising organic composition of capital, and, finally, in his classic formulation of the so-called "materialist conception of history," the growth of the "productive forces."

THE GROWTH OF THE PRODUCTIVE FORCES UNDER CAPITALISM: PRODUCTIVITY, EXPLOITATION AND ALIENATION

In the debate on *alienation* of recent years, there are those who maintain that it is pure myth-making to argue that this problem continued to occupy Marx's attention throughout his life.[24] Thus Daniel Bell, for example, speaks of a "young" and an "old" Marx, the younger having been interested in alienation, and the older having abandoned the concept as entirely too romantic and politically ineffective. In the discussion that follows it will be seen that far from abandoning the concept in his later years, Marx refined it and treated it as an objective process.

Marx employed distinct terms to describe this process: *Entausserung* and *Entfremdung*. The first term referred to the externalization of human powers during the process of production and the pouring of those powers into material objects, e.g., commodities. This externalization also referred to the productive forces which the workers had created but over which they were increasingly losing control. The second term, *Entfremdung*—denoting the *subjective* development that was at least in part a consequence of the first—referred to the *estrangement* of man from man.

The main points which the following discussion seeks to demonstrate are: (a) that Marx continued to be concerned with the problem of alienation throughout his life; (b) that he linked alienation to the growth of productive forces under capitalism, a precondition of man's eventual freedom which in the meantime was alienating man's creative and reflective powers; (c) that he linked it also to the concept of *exploitation* which disclosed the sources of the capitalist's revenue and its important function in the growth of the productive forces; and, finally, (d) that Marx viewed alienation not as a consequence of technology *qua* technology—but of technology under capitalism. Here it will be seen that Bell is wrong when he asserts that except for literary and illustrative references in *Capital,* Marx did not give attention to the dehumanization of labor and the fragmentation of work.[25] Marx did *not* gloss over this problem. On the contrary he analyzed it painstakingly and in the spirit of scientific inquiry. However, because he did this in close connection with two other problems, namely, productivity and exploitation, it *is* possible to get a different impression. With these comments in mind, the way in which Marx addressed himself to the three problems will become more clear.

Cooperation, for Marx, may be viewed as the first phase in the development of the productive forces within the capitalist mode of production. Although cooperation is characteristic of all production on a large scale, it prevails under capitalism in those branches of production in which capital operates on a large scale, but division of labor and machinery play a subordinate part. "A greater number of laborers working together, at the same time, in one place, in order to produce the same sort of commodity under the mastership of one capitalist, constitutes, both historically and logically, the starting point of capitalist production." [26] Cooperation of this kind takes place mainly in manufacture in the strict sense, i.e., hand-production, and is hardly distinguished in its early stages from handicraft production in the guilds. The main difference lies in the larger number of workers simultaneously employed by one and the same capitalist.

This kind of "simple" cooperation, even unaccompanied by new instruments of production, effects a change in the material conditions of production. To employ twenty weavers instead of one, even while using conventional looms, requires a workshop large enough to accommodate the twenty and thus requires an expansion of the means of production. The bringing together of these workers side by side, even while they are engaged in the same process, increases their productive power. Marx illustrates this with the enhanced striking power of a military unit under conditions of cooperation. Just as the offensive power of a squadron or regiment is essentially different from the sum of the offensive powers of the individual soldiers taken separately, ". . . so the sum total of the mechanical forces exerted by isolated workmen differs from the social force that is developed, when many hands take part simultaneously in one and the same undivided operation, such as raising a heavy weight, turning a winch or removing an obstacle." [27] The emphasis here is on the *socially* productive force that comes into being by bringing the many men together. The capitalist pays each individual worker for his individual labor-power and gets more than he bargained for. He now gains directly from their cooperation for he could not have gained as much surplus-value by employing 12 isolated men, each working 12 hours, as 12 working together and cooperating for 12 hours. In addition, without anyone realizing it, the extension of the scale of production together with the contraction of the "arena," i.e., assembling many workers under one roof, provide the requisite conditions for the further development of "productive forces"—a consequence impossible when the workers and the means of production are isolated and scattered as in the cottage system, for example.

For Marx, cooperation in this form characterized the earliest phase of capitalism and was an important new productive force. It was new not in the sense that there were no examples of simple cooperation before in history, but in the sense that the utilization and further growth of this productive force was now dependent on specific *relations of production*. The existence of large outlays of capital now became a precondition for the cooperation of many workers. The workers could not cooperate unless they were employed simultaneously by the same capitalist.

In the specific case of English capitalism in the period under consideration, the requisite "relations of production" did exist— capitalists with adequate means of production and money, on the one hand, and workers without either, on the other. In this phase the "relations of production" had not yet become fetters, and the "productive forces" had not yet come in conflict with them. On the contrary, the existing relations provided the framework within which the productive forces could continue to develop. The concentration of the means of production in the hands of the capitalists became the precondition for the cooperation of many workers; the extent of their cooperation depended on the extent of concentration; the whole process rested on capitalist relations of production, or property relations.

Once the scale of cooperation attains certain dimensions, the capitalist assumes a dual role. In part this role is indispensable to the process of production and a requirement of it. In part, however, the role is a function of the exploitative relationship between capitalist and worker. In his first role Marx compares the owner to the general on the battle-field, or the conductor of a symphony orchestra. "All combined labor on a large scale requires, more or less, a directing authority, in order to secure the harmonious working of the individual activities, and to perform the general functions that have their origin in the action of the combined organism . . . . A single violin player is his own conductor; an orchestra requires a separate one."[28] In his other role, however, the owner may be compared with an overseer, whose disciplinary function flows not from the social character of the labor-process but from his main aim in the process, i.e., extracting surplus-value. The control of the capitalist is therefore two-fold because of the two-fold character of the process of production itself. On the one hand, it is a social process for producing use-values and, on the other, it is a process for creating surplus-value. With the growing scale of production the capitalist soon relinquishes his supervisory function as earlier he was relieved of any actual labor. In his place there appears a special kind of worker whose main job it becomes to supervise others. The managers, foremen, etc., command in the name of the capitalist.

Marx therefore distinguished two different functions of the capitalist—the entrepreneurial as opposed to the supervisory or, what is today distinguished as the coordinative, decision-making functions of management as opposed to the merely supervisory. The distinction is also important for an understanding of his concept of "productive forces." Marx would have included in this concept the function of coordination made necessary by the co-operative character of the labor process. Not so with the different type of "control," which is necessitated by the capitalist character of the process, and the conflict of interests which he saw between capitalist and worker. Marx made this point by saying, "It is not because he is a leader of industry that a man is a capitalist; on the contrary, he is a leader of industry because he is a capitalist." [29] Thus the second type of function, control and supervision, was an attribute of capital, of the capitalist system. It appeared indispensable and indeed was so as long as the capitalist relations of production prevailed. On the other hand, the coordinative function Marx viewed as an attribute of all social production; this required a certain level of education, skills, and experience and was therefore an integral part of the developing "productive forces." These forces were indeed expanding and were described by Marx as a more complex form of cooperation, namely, *division of labor in manufacture*. This was the second phase in the growth of the productive forces under capitalism.

Division of Labor in Manufacture

As compared with simple cooperation, manufacture is based on a more complex division of labor. This arises in two ways: (1) by bringing together in one workshop and under the control of one capitalist workers of various independent handicrafts; and (2) by the reverse of this, namely, by employing in one workshop a number of craftsmen who all do the same kind of work. In the first case each worker contributes by his particular and different skill to one commodity, e.g., tailors, locksmiths, and other craftsmen are now exclusively occupied in carriage-making. In the second case, each worker, being from the same craft, makes the commodity in its entirety. Eventually, of course, instead of each man performing all the various operations in succession, these operations are changed into disconnected, isolated ones, carried on side by side. Each operation is assigned to a different artisan, and all the operations are performed simultaneously by the new cooperative organization.

Manufacture therefore arises out of handicrafts, in one case uniting the formerly independent ones and in the other uniting the members of the same craft. It is this uniting of the crafts, forging them into one productive organization whose parts are *human beings,* which distinguishes manufacture as a new phase in the growth of productive forces. This phase retains the character of handicraft because each operation is still performed by hand and is therefore dependent on the skill and dexterity of the individual workman in handling his tools.

Since he is now engaged in the same simple operation, however, the worker begins to lose some of the creative prerogatives he exercised before. His whole body becomes an "automatic, specialized implement of that operation." [30] What he loses in creativity he gains in efficiency. This worker takes less time in doing the operation than the craftsman who performs the entire series of operations in succession. The division of labor among many such workers is the basis of the productive system called manufacture, a new organization of labor under which the socially

productive power of labor is increased. This new productive force
under the capitalist system is gained in manufacture by concen-
trating the powers already existing in the *society at large*. Thus
manufacture, according to Marx, ". . . produces the skill of
the detail laborer, by reproducing, and systematically driving to
an extreme within the workshop, the naturally developed differentiation of trades which it found ready to hand in society at
large." [31]

The capitalist entrepreneur had already discovered at this early
stage of development that anything which interrupts the "constant
flow" of the labor-process also cuts into his profits. The production
of commodities with a minimum of labor time, not a consideration
at all under the guild system, now became a consideration of
central importance. Decreasing the labor time necessary for the
production of commodities was impossible so long as the worker
had to perform a series of fractional operations which required
him at one time to change his place and at another to change his
tools. These shifts interrupted the flow by creating gaps in the
working day which had to be closed by tying the worker to one
and the same operation for the entire day. For Marx the closing
of these gaps which manufacture achieved resulted in a further
increase in the productive power of labor, in the productive forces
under capitalism.

The concentration of production, of the various skills and
trades in one workshop, also made necessary changes in the tools
employed. Unlike the craftsman who used a few tools for many
operations, the worker now employed a specialized tool for each
specialized operation. Marx expressed this succinctly: "Manufacture is characterized by the differentiation of the instruments of
labor—a differentiation whereby implements of a given sort ac-
quire fixed shapes, adapted to each particular application, and by
the specialization of those instruments, giving to each special
implement its full play only in the hands of a specific detail
laborer." [32]

Thus the manufacturing period increased the variety of tools
by adapting them to the special function of each detail laborer.
This development is important to Marx for a number of reasons.
In itself it constituted a further revolutionizing of the forces of

production. In addition it was effecting radical changes in the world of work. Old social forms were decomposing and their fragments becoming parts of a new social organization of work. This fragmentation, and the consequent transformation of the worker into a detail laborer, could not take place, Marx believed, without at the same time causing significant changes in the worker's character and personality. The process was alienating the worker from his creative powers and making him a tool-user requiring less reflective and creative power than before. This phenomenon, as it later became crystal-clear with machine production, became one basis for Marx's indictment of the capitalist system. Equally important is the fact that the fragmentation of the labor process which took place with manufacture created the social conditions for the introduction of *machinery*. The process leading to the introduction of machinery is interesting for the light it throws on the world of work and its changing functions, and for the changes which provided the basis for modern industry.

In the manufacturing period proper, machinery played a small and sporadic role. Not machinery but division of labor was the central characteristic of this phase. Although the principle of decreasing the necessary labor time in the production of commodities was recognized by the capitalists, it was accomplished chiefly by the greater division of labor. The employment of machinery was the exception and occurred in certain simple first processes which had to be carried out on a large scale and with the application of great force.

In the case of manufacture, the "collective laborer," the organization formed by the combination of a number of detail laborers, is the "machinery" characteristic of it. The higher productivity of this organization is made possible precisely by the separation and isolation of the various operations and the workers performing them. The workers are divided, classified, and grouped according to their very specific functions. What is taken away from the individual worker in skill, creativity, and reflective powers, is given to the organization. The deficiencies of the former become the virtues of the latter. The organization as a whole is enriched by alienating the worker from his individual powers.

Moreover, manufacture develops a hierarchy of labor. If the

workers are now tied to limited functions, these are parts in a hierarchy and are parceled out among them according to their socially acquired capabilities. At the very bottom of the hierarchy are those who perform the simplest manipulations of which every man is capable. Hence, in contrast with guild production, manufacture brings into being a class of so-called unskilled workers, a class unknown in handicraft production. Describing this change, Marx wrote: "If it [manufacturing] develops a one-sided specialty into a perfection, at the expense of the whole of a man's working capacity, it also begins to make a specialty of the absence of all development. Alongside the hierarchic gradation there steps the simple separation of the laborers into skilled and unskilled." [33]

The Capitalistic Character of Manufacture

Division of labor in society as a whole was common to all previous modes of production. In Western society, however, the division of labor in the workshop as practiced in manufacture was, in Marx's view, a special creation of the capitalist mode of production. As in the case of cooperation this first appeared in manufacture as an increased number of laborers under the control of one capitalist. But the division of labor in manufacture made this increase in the number of workers a technical necessity, and made the workers completely dependent upon the capitalist.

For example, the minimum number of workers that a capitalist can employ is determined by the previously established division of labor. Additional gains in efficiency are obtainable only by adding multiples of the various detail groups. This increase in the *variable component of capital* also requires an increase in the constant component, in workshops, implements, etc., and especially in raw material, the need for which increases at a faster ratio than the number of workers. From this Marx concludes that the

> . . . quantity of it [raw material] consumed in a given time, by a given amount of labor, increases in the same ratio as does the productive power of that labor in consequence of its division. Hence, it is a law, based on the very nature of manufacture, that the minimum amount of capital, which is bound to be in the hands of each capitalist, must keep increasing; in other words, that the transformation into capital of the social means of production and subsistence must keep extending.[34]

Marx is intent upon showing the growth in the socially productive power of labor, its dependence upon capitalist property relations, and the price which the individual worker pays for this increased productivity. The main tendencies of the capitalist system assert themselves in this period. First, the expansion of capital simultaneous with its concentration into increasingly larger units is already clear in the manufacturing phase. Second, this together with the fragmentation of the old crafts and the conversion of craftsmen into detail laborers has the consequence of alienating the reflective and creative faculties from the worker and transferring them to the organization of which he is a part. Knowledge, judgment, and will, which previously had been exercised in so small a degree by the individual craftsman now become a function of the productive organization as a whole. The rationality lost by the detail laborers is now exercised by the entrepreneur within his workshop. The exercise of rationality by the worker is no longer required in an eminently rational process. The worker is "brought face to face with the intellectual potencies of the material process of production, as the property of another, and as a ruling power." [35] The process which began in simple cooperation, where the capitalist represented to the worker the power and will of associated labor, became more pronounced in manufacture which reduced the worker to a detail laborer.

To summarize, manufacture, the second phase in the developing forces of production, rested on the decomposition of handicrafts, the specialization of the instruments of labor, the formation of detail laborers, and the grouping and combining of the latter in a single productive organization. This organization provided for a qualitatively higher productivity of labor and thus constituted a growth in the productive forces of the society. The newer social division of labor now allowed for the production of more commodities with a given quantity of labor-power, hence for the cheapening of commodities, and for the acceleration in the accumulation of capital.

Yet manufacture was limited. Typically its technical basis was still craft-production, the hand tool. This narrow technical basis came into conflict with the requirements of production which manufacture itself created. One of the important creations of this phase was the workshop for the production of the instruments of labor themselves. In Marx's words: "This workshop, the product of the division of labor in manufacture, produced in turn—machines. It is they that sweep away the handicraftsman's work as the regulating principle of social production." [36] It is machinery and modern industry that constitute the third phase in the growing productive forces under capitalism. Before exploring the next phase, however, a few points made by Marx up to this point should be made more explicit.

First, it should be noted that the productive forces were developing long before the widespread application of machinery in industry, i.e., long before the industrial revolution. Second, it was the social organization of labor as it took shape in the manufacturing phase, particularly in the *workshop,* which provided the basis for the introduction of machinery. Third, the conflict which Marx saw in this phase between the "productive forces" and the "relations of production" was due to the inadequate technical basis of manufacturing. The existing framework of social organization required a different technical basis. This indicated for Marx that the existing property relations provided for the further accelerated growth of the productive forces within the system. This is quite different from the later phenomenon where machine-industry as a productive force conflicts with existing (bourgeois) property relations. This conflict in the third phase, as it became manifest in crises of overproduction, constituted for Marx the necessary, if not sufficient, condition for the change *of* the system. This will become clearer in our later discussion of Marx's theory. It remains for us to consider the third and final phase of Marx's conception of the capitalist mode of production.

Machinery and Modern Industry

Marx opens his discussion of machinery with a quotation from John Stuart Mill. "It is questionable if all the mechanical inventions yet made have lightened the day's toil of any human being." And in a footnote Marx characteristically adds: "Mill should have said, 'Of any human being not fed by other people's labor,' for, without doubt, machinery has greatly increased the number of well-to-do idlers." [37] Mill's observation was based on the capitalist system and in that system the lightening of human toil was by no means the aim of the application of machinery. Rather, its application was intended to lower costs of production and thereby to produce greater surplus-value which the capitalist could then appropriate as he wished. If in manufacture the revolution in the mode of production began with the organization of labor-power, in modern industry it began with the instruments of production.

Machinery and its employment in modern industry is the most important phase in the development of the capitalist mode of production. In its inception it rests squarely on manufacture and transforms hand tools into "working machines." The working machine or *tool,* is one of three parts of any modern machine which includes the motor mechanism and the transmitting mechanism. This tool was generally an adaptation of those used by the handicraftsmen or manufacturing workmen and for a long time was actually manufactured by these workers. It was then fitted into the body of the machine. The machine proper is a mechanism which once in motion performs with its tools the same operations that were formerly done by the workman with similar tools. Thus the machine, the starting point of the industrial revolution, increasingly supersedes the worker. This was the beginning of a central tendency of the capitalist system—the increasing displacement and supersession of men by machines.

With the increase in the size of the machine and the number of its working tools, a more massive moving power than man was required to drive it. Horsepower and water power could serve as only temporary solutions under the conditions of an expanding industrial system. The former was an unsatisfactory form of power due to its costliness and its restricted application in factories. The use of the latter was also beset with difficulties. It could be neither increased nor decreased at will, was not available during certain seasons of the year and, above all, was only a local source of power.

The invention which provided the "breakthrough" and made it possible to transcend local conditions was Watt's so-called double-acting steam engine. It generated its own power by consuming coal and water, and was mobile; it permitted production to be concentrated in towns instead of being scattered in the country like the water-wheels. The social significance of this new machine therefore lay not so much in its specific function but in its universal applicability; industry was no longer bound to particular locales. The increasing application of such machines brought about even greater contrasts in working conditions as compared with previous phases.

If, with manufacture, the productive process is adapted to the skills of the worker, with the machine-system, the worker is compelled to adapt to the process. The subjective principle now disappears and the whole process is examined objectively. Production is analyzed into a sequence of phases and each phase is carried out by means of machines. The total system is now considered superior the more the process becomes a continuous one, the less it is interrupted in its various phases, the more the shifts from one phase to another are made not by hand, but by machinery.

Some Effects of Machinery on the Workman

Marx's criticisms of machine industry under capitalism are well-known. The employment of women and children in harsh industrial tasks, the lengthening of the working day and, when eventually shortened, the intensification of labor by speed-up, etc., pointed up the basically anti-human character of the system. In his examination of the development of the capitalist mode of production, he was among the first to describe in detail the changing role of the worker and the effect of the machine upon him. He described, for example, how the old system of division of labor, while being thrown overboard by machinery, still hung on in the factory in an even "more hideous form." "The life-long specialty of handling one and the same tool, now becomes the life-long specialty of serving one and the same machine." [38] In this way the worker's dependence upon the factory, and therefore on the capitalist, is rendered complete. In manufacture the worker used the tool; in the factory the machine uses him. Under these circumstances the intellectual powers of the worker become superfluous; his special skills become of little importance and even vanish before the gigantic physical forces of the total factory organization and the hidden mind behind it all. Small wonder that in the earliest period of machine production the worker saw the cause of his troubles in the machine itself, and revolted against the machine and the system based upon it.

But there is still another consequence of machine industry:

If it be said that 100 millions of people would be required in England to spin with the old spinning-wheel the cotton that is now spun with mules by 500,000 people, this does not mean that the mules took the place of those millions who never existed. It means only this, that many millions of workpeople would be required to replace the spinning machinery. If, on the other hand, we say, that in England the power-loom threw 800,000 weavers on the streets, we do not refer to existing machinery, that would have to be replaced by a definite number of workpeople, but to a number of weavers in existence who were actually replaced or displaced by the loom.[39]

This is the basis of the antagonism between the machine and the worker under capitalism. The machine becomes a competitor of the worker himself. The expansion of machine production is directly proportional to the number of workers rendered superfluous by the machinery. With the loss of his function—or with the loss of the use-value of his labor-power as Marx would express it—the worker loses also his exchange-value. He becomes unsalable! The superfluous workers become a reserve army of unemployed who swamp the labor market and depress wages even below the subsistence level.

Already in his time Marx saw the relative decline in production workers due to the extraordinary productiveness of modern industry. Simultaneous with this decline he also saw the growth in the "unproductive" employment of an increasingly large part of the working class. The British census of 1861 revealed the size of the servant class at 1,208,648. Marx observed that "All the persons employed in textile factories and in mines, taken together, number 1,208,442; those employed in textile factories and metal industries, taken together, number 1,039,605; in both cases less than the number of domestic slaves. What a splendid result of the capitalist exploitation of machinery."[40] In spite of this tendency— since Marx lived in a period of the rapid expansion of capitalism—he believed that the workers would grow in absolute terms and become the most numerous class. This was one of the reasons why he considered it the revolutionary class under capitalism and the agency by which the system would be changed.

For Marx the third phase in the development of the capitalist mode of production is therefore the *critical* one. During this phase modern industry accelerates the concentration of capital and leads to the prominence of the factory system. It increasingly destroys all the previous forms of production and replaces them by the modern capitalist form, by the direct and open power of capital. But the process which leads to the power of capital leads also to ". . . the contradictions and antagonisms of the capitalist form of production, and thereby provides, along with the elements for the formation of a new society, the forces for exploding the old one." [41]

It is clear that for Marx the development of productive forces under capitalism is at once the social and technical basis of man's eventual emancipation and, ironically enough, a manifestation of man's growing alienation. Man is increasingly losing control of the productive process. Only by forfeiting more and more of his creativity at work does the worker contribute to the growth and efficiency of the productive organization. Far from having deserted the concept of alienation, then, Marx sharpened and concretized it by studying it as an objective process in the world of work.

Marx linked the concept of alienation to another which had become important to him—exploitation. Since this meant the extraction of surplus-value from the labor of the workers and since surplus-value, reinvested in the expansion of the productive organization, was the basis of the growth of the productive forces, the connection between exploitation and alienation which Marx made becomes clear. Exploitation itself is a form of alienation and is inherent in the capitalist-worker relationship; alienation is not the consequence of industrial development *per se,* but of industrial development under capitalism.

NOTES

1. T. B. Bottomore and Maximilien Rubel, *Karl Marx: Selected Writings in Sociology and Social Philosophy.* London: Watts & Co., 1961, p. 17.

2. Karl Marx, *Economic and Philosophic Manuscripts.* Translated by T. B. Bottomore in Erich Fromm's *Marx's Concept of Man.* New York: Frederick Ungar Publishing Co., 1961, p. 130. These manuscripts are hereafter cited as E.P.M.

3. Bottomore and Rubel, *op. cit.*, p. 21.

4. For an illuminating discussion of this point see Paul M. Sweezy, *The Theory of Capitalist Development*. New York: Monthly Review Press, 1956, pp. 11-20.

5. *Ibid.*, p. 11.

6. Karl Marx, *Capital* Vol I. Moscow: Foreign Languages Publishing House, 1954, p. 8.

7. These social relations are reintroduced at a later stage of analysis, i.e., in Vols. II and III of *Capital*.

8. Sweezy, *op. cit.*, p. 17.

9. Marx, *Capital* Vol. I, p. 8.

10. *Ibid.*, p. 94.

11. *Ibid.*, p. 714.

12. *Ibid.*, p. 716.

13. *Ibid.*, p. 718.

14. *Ibid.*, p. 719.

15. *Ibid.*, p. 167.

16. Engels, "Speech at the Graveside of Karl Marx," in Karl Marx and Frederick Engels, *Selected Works* Vol. II. Moscow: Foreign Languages Publishing House, 1950, p. 151. Hereafter cited as MESW.

17. Marx, *Capital* Vol. I, p. 167.

18. *Ibid.*, p. 171.

19. *Ibid.*, p. 192.

20. *Ibid.*, p. 192.

21. *Ibid.*, p. 195.

22. Karl Marx, *Communist Manifesto*. London: George Allen and Unwin Ltd., 1948, p. 129.

23. See *Capital* Vol. I, Ch. VIII, pp. 199-211.

24. For an account of the debate and a statement of this position see Daniel Bell, "The Debate on Alienation," pp. 195-214, in *Revisionism: Essays on the History of Marxist Ideas*. Edited by Leopold Labedz. New York: Frederick A. Praeger, 1962.

25. See Bell's discussion in *Ibid.*, p. 204.

26. Marx, *Capital* Vol. I, p. 322.

27. *Ibid.*, p. 326.

28. *Ibid.*, pp. 330-331.

29. *Ibid.*, p. 332.

30. *Ibid.*, p. 339.

31. *Ibid.*, p. 339.

32. *Ibid.*, p. 341.

33. *Ibid.*, p. 350.

34. *Ibid.*, pp. 359-360.

35. *Ibid.*, p. 361.

36. *Ibid.*, p. 368.

37. *Ibid.*, p. 371.

38. *Ibid.*, p. 422.
39. *Ibid.*, p. 429.
40. *Ibid.*, p. 447.
41. *Ibid.*, p. 503.

III. Marx's Theory of the Capitalist System

MARX'S CONCEPTION OF THE CAPITALIST SYSTEM, PARTICULARLY its mode of production, has been carefully explored. His model provides us with the essential elements to which attention must be paid if we are to understand the system and how it changes. In Marx's model the elements are not left to interact in some vague and eclectic way. They are built into the model in explicit interconnections with one another and causal weights are assigned to each of them. These interconnections and weights are Marx's specific theoretical propositions which combine to make up his most general social theory: the theory of social change and the role of revolution within it. In this part our concern will be first to present and explicate Marx's theories and then critically to evaluate them.

For Marx the labor-process, the labor activity of real men, was the fundamental human activity. In his analysis of the workings of capitalism, Marx posited labor activity, or production, as the most important sphere of social conduct within the system. In all his discussions of the process of production Marx emphasized the two-fold character of human relations in that process. On the one hand, human beings enter into a relation with nature but, on the other hand, not only with nature. Marx wrote that men produce only by

> . . . cooperating in a certain way and mutually exchanging their activities. In order to produce they enter into definite connections and relations with one other and only within these social connections and relations does their action on nature, does production take place.

These social relations into which the producers enter with one another, the conditions under which they exchange their activities and participate in the whole act of production, will naturally vary according to the character of the means of production.[1]

Marx illustrated the latter point—that relations vary with the means of production—saying, "Labour is organized, is divided differently according to the instruments it disposes over. The hand-mill presupposes a different division of labour from the steam-mill."[2] Working toward a scientific conception of social systems and their operation, Marx centered his attention on two basic elements: The relationship of men with nature as mediated by instruments of production which he called "productive forces," and the social relations among the men themselves, which he called "relations of production." "The social relations within which individuals produce, *the social relations of production, change, are transformed, with the change and development of the material means of production, the productive forces. The relations of production in their totality constitute what are called the social relations, society, and, specifically, a society at a definite stage of historical development,* a society with a peculiar, distinctive character."[3] (Italics in original.) Thus Marx viewed productive forces as the independent variable, and *relations of production* as the dependent one. Although no hard and fast lines could be drawn between the stages in the development of societies, at least three such stages, or different types of society, could be delineated in human history. "Ancient society, feudal society, bourgeois (or capitalist) society, are such totalities of relations of production, each of which denotes a particular stage of development in the history of mankind."[4] Marx was moving toward a precise definition of terms in his major theoretical proposition but had not yet achieved it. For these definitions, as compared with later refinements which Marx introduced, fall down at two points. First, Marx's definition of "productive forces" is inaccurate in this formulation because he equates them with the material means of production. That these concepts are neither interchangeable nor coterminous should be clear from our recent discussion of the capitalist mode of production in which it was seen that cooperation itself is a *productive force*. Secondly, Marx was imprecise in equating the totality of productive relations with society as a whole. A decade later he refined the definition so that the totality of productive relations constitutes not society as a whole, but the *most important sphere of social conduct within society, the foundation of all other social relations of society.*

The most precise and therefore most often quoted statement concerning the fundamentals of a social system is found in Marx's preface to *A Contribution to the Critique of Political Economy.* It will serve as a basis for the analysis of the key terms in Marx's general theory.

> In the social production which men carry on they enter into definite relations that are indispensable and independent of their will; these relations of production correspond to a definite stage of development of their material powers of production. *The sum total of these relations of production constitutes the economic structure* of society—the real foundation, on which rise legal and political superstructures and to which correspond definite forms of social consciousness. The mode of production in material life determines the general character of the social, political and spiritual processes of life. It is not the consciousness of men that determines their existence, but, on the contrary, their social existence determines their consciousness. At a certain stage of their development, the material forces of production in society come in conflict with the existing relations of production, or—what is but a legal expression for the same thing—with the property relations within which they had been at work before. From forms of development of the forces of production these relations turn into their fetters. Then comes the period of social revolution. With the change of the economic foundation the entire immense superstructure is more or less rapidly transformed.[5] (Italics mine.)

The italicized sentence indicates a sharper conceptualization of social structure and it is thus an improvement over Marx's previous formulation. Here the totality of productive relations is seen as constituting not society as a whole but the economic structure of society, the foundation of the other spheres in society. Although Marx's statement is not an ambiguous one, at least one term in these propositions does have a vague meaning and requires clarification.

When Marx speaks of the *productive forces* in society coming in conflict with the existing *relations of production,* he equates the latter with property relations. Yet, when he speaks of the totality of relations of production as the economic structure, he clearly means something more than this. In exploring the phases of development from simple cooperation to machinery and modern industry, it was seen how older social relations in the sphere of production were dissolved and supplanted by new ones. The social relations which had changed in this process were the social relations at work. According to Marx's view, however, the basic property relations of the system as a whole had remained unchanged, i.e., the changes from cooperation to machine production had taken place within the framework of capitalist property relations. Therefore, in considering Marx's theory, clarity requires that an important distinction be made between the two types of *social relations of production*. These may be called: (a) *formal-legal relations of production* and (b) *work-relations*. These two types of relations point to the two-fold character which Marx may have intended to assign to his concept "relations of production," but which he never developed explicitly. The *formal-legal relations of production* refer to the socially defined rights of access of individuals to the productive resources: who owns and controls the means of making a living and who does not. These relations determine how the results of the productive process will be shared. In these terms the guild system, the cottage system and the factory system specify the different conditions under which individuals may enter the productive process and their rights to share in its results. These *formal-legal relations* which characterize each system are therefore equivalent to Marx's concept of *property-relations,* a concept which must be distinguished from *work-relations*. This term refers to the social relationships which men enter while cooperating in the process of production. These relationships are directly determined by the division of labor and technology of a particular productive process so that the type of relationship accompanying the use of hand tools will be quite different from that accompanying machine production. Moreover, *work-relations,* more often than not, are direct, and involve the workers in face-to-face associations.

The two types of relationships are connected with each other in a variety of ways. For instance, whether *formal-legal relations of production* and *work-relations* will or will not involve the same individuals depends on the nature of the productive system. In a simple agricultural society the two types of social relationships are often combined. A son works not only *for* his father but *with* him in the process of production. Typically this is not true of the industrial system, particularly in its later phases, where the *formal-legal relations* are rarely combined with the *work-relations*.

Another important observation about the two types of relationships is that while *formal-legal relations* tend to determine a certain set of *work-relations,* the two often vary independently. Under the formal relationships of the capitalist system men have formed the most varied types of social relationships with their fellow workers. The *work-relations* during the manufacturing phase, for example, were quite different from those under conditions of machinery and modern industry. Yet, for Marx the workers were subject in the respective periods to the same capitalist property relations. Conversely, as was seen in the transition from guild production to simple cooperation, although the formal property-relations changed—from guildmasters to capitalists—the social relations at work changed hardly at all. Hence it can be seen that the two types of relationship vary somewhat independently, and at different rates. The *work-relations* change much more rapidly and frequently than the *formal* or *property-relationships.* For Marx, owing to the level of abstraction at which he was considering "modes of production," only a few, perhaps four or five, different types of *formal-legal relationships* had existed in history. *Work-relations,* in contrast, are extremely variable since they are based on technological conditions which are subject to frequent change. Clearly, these are important distinctions for an understanding of Marx's theoretical propositions.

What then is the significance in Marx's theory of *property-relations?* They determine the source of power in the productive system—ownership, control and direction. Under capitalism, this is a fact of fundamental importance; for depending on whether one owns the "means of production" or not, one's life-chances vary accordingly. The class structure of society is a function of its property-relations and the fate of a man tends to be determined by the class into which he is born. *Property-relations* is therefore an important concept in Marx's theory of social classes; but it is also essential, as we shall see, for an understanding of his theory of social change.

In contrast with *property-relations,* the significance of *work-*

relations becomes clear from the following discussion in which Marx definitely points to them. "By social we understand the co-operation of several individuals, no matter under what conditions, in what manner and to what end. It follows from this that a certain mode of production, or industrial stage, is always combined with a certain mode of cooperation, or social stage, and *this mode of cooperation is itself a 'productive force.'* " [6] (Italics mine.) One essential point, then, in the distinction between the two types of relationship, is that *work-relations* constitute an integral part of the *productive forces* of a society.

There is therefore nothing mystical or metaphysical in the term *productive forces* as used by Marx. It includes, first of all, the real labor-power of working men. It is the social force of these living workers by which they produce the means of satisfying the social needs of their existence; it therefore includes these workers, the means of production employed by them and the definite form of social cooperation conditioned by the means of production. Anything which increases the productivity of human labor power increases the "productive forces" of a society. Thus while this concept denotes men's mastery of nature as expressed in the advance of technique and science, the concept includes something more. It includes the social organization of production itself, i.e., the cooperation and division of labor among men which in this study has been designated as *work-relations*.

This interaction of men with nature and with one another, which constitutes the developing *productive forces* of a society, takes place within the framework of existing *property-relations*. In the early phase of a system's development, the *property-relations* facilitate the constant growth of the productive forces, including the changing *work-relations*. In the later phases of the system's development, however, the productive forces are retarded and hampered in their growth by the very same *property-relations*. These have to be "burst asunder" in order to allow for the further expansion of the productive forces. The workers, acting as a class, set free the forces potentially existing in social labor by their revolutionary action. In this sense the workers' revolution is a constructive act because it frees the productive forces of restraints. By their revolution, the workers eliminate the restraints imposed by capitalist *property-relations* on social productivity. Marx's theory is therefore not merely technological. The tension between productive forces and *property-relations* is not a mere lack of adjustment between technical innovations and their social application. According to Marx's theory, it is impossible to measure accurately the productive forces of a society apart from the *formal-legal relations* in which they are at work; it is impossible to measure productive forces purely in terms of natural science and technology. At best one can make only a reasonable estimate of the potential of a given technology under different property-relations. Mere technical prescriptions are therefore inadequate in order to "unfetter" the productive forces. Karl Korsch presents Marx's view thus: "There is more power of resistance in the mute force of economic conditions and in the economically and politically organized forces of the class interested in the maintenance of those conditions than well-meaning technocrats have ever dreamt of." [7]

Thus, Marx divided the "mode of production" into two parts: static property-relations and dynamic productive forces. The property-relations either advance or block the growth of the productive forces. The potential of these forces cannot be measured by a technological calculation alone. The potential can be released only by the elimination of the relations which hamper them. With the removal of these property-relations and the establishment of newer and more flexible ones, the further development of the productive forces and new forms of human activity again become possible. The "mode of production" changes as developing productive forces effect changes in the formal relations of production; as the "mode of production" changes, other spheres of social conduct, or subsystems, e.g., legal, political, ideological, change in consequence. Thus stated, there is nothing ambiguous about this theory. It unequivocally asserts that a society's changing economic structure determines changes in the social structure as a whole, as well as in the consciousness of the people within it.

Some Marxists have tried to defend Marx from the apparent economic determinism of his theory. Basing themselves on some of Engels' letters, [8] in which he spoke of the superstructure acting back upon the foundation, they posit the interplay of various factors. They thus oppose to Marx's theory a vague eclecticism by which everything interacts with everything and no causal sequence is determinable. This interpretation is not justified by the content of Engels' letters. For while he admits to the inter-action of factors, he also insists that the economic factor always asserts itself in the so-called "final analysis." Granting the ques-tion-begging character of the phrase, "final analysis," and the difficulties it raises, Engels' formulation may still be interpreted in two ways: (a) "economic determinism" in the *long run,* and (b) pluralistic interaction of factors in the *short run.* The *time* factor, then, becomes very important in Marx's theory; and since Marx derived this generalization from his studies of the long-run eco-nomic developments in western Europe, it is clear why "economic necessity," as Engels called it, did indeed appear—in that con-text—ultimately to assert itself. The evidence clearly suggests that Marx was making this generalization not about all societies and all periods—not about the Orient, for example—but about a special case: The changes in the "mode of production" which began to occur during the late middle ages and especially from the 16th century in England and certain other countries of western Europe. In this connection, Marx wrote: "The so-called primitive accumulation, therefore, is nothing else than the historical process of divorcing the producer from the means of production. It ap-pears as primitive, because it forms the prehistoric stage of capital and of the mode of production corresponding with it." [9] In con-cluding his discussion, Marx leaves no doubt that he was *not* laying down a general law: "Although we come across the first beginnings of capitalist production as early as the 14th or 15th century, sporadically, in certain towns of the Mediterranean, the capitalistic era dates from the 16th century . . . . The history of this expropriation, in different countries, assumes different aspects, and runs through its various phases in different orders of succes-sion, and at different periods. In England alone, which we take as our example, has it the classic form." [10]

The historically specific character of Marx's theory may be seen more clearly from his description of the concrete changes which took place in western Europe with the development of the capitalist mode of production. These changes were dramatically summarized in the *Communist Manifesto.* In the following sum-mary and discussion the extent to which Marx based his generaliza-tions on empirical-historical data from *west-European history,* and that history alone, should become perfectly clear. Of course, this fact does not in any way preclude the employment of Marx's general propositions as working hypotheses in the study of other societies and other periods. Indeed, as we shall see in a later discussion, this may very well be the most valuable part of his legacy, particularly for the study of macrodynamics, or whole societies in the process of change.

In the following section, the empirical-historical and theoretical statements which Marx formulated in the *Communist Manifesto*,[11] are enumerated and, wherever deemed necessary, commented upon. Afterwards, the major modifications of his theory, which Marx introduced in the light of the historical experience from 1848 to 1871, will be considered. This will be followed by a critical discussion of Marx's major theoretical propositions.

1. Pre-capitalist as well as capitalist societies have been characterized by class struggle.

When once the productivity of labor in a society has attained the point where it can yield a surplus product over and above the subsistence requirements of the producers, a group other than the producers themselves finds ways of appropriating the surplus. Periodically, and in various forms, a conflict ensues for rights of control of this surplus.

2. Modern capitalist society has set up new classes in place of old.

A major tendency of capitalist society is its polarization into two hostile and directly opposed classes: bourgeoisie and proletariat.

3. The change from the feudal to the capitalist system was not a consequence of solely internal causes.

The following passage, for example, clearly indicates that factors external to the system were taken into account by Marx: "The East Indian and the Chinese markets, the colonization of America, trade with the colonies, and multiplication of the means of exchange and of commodities in general, gave an unprecedented impetus to commerce, navigation, and manufacturing industry, thus fostering the growth of the revolutionary element [the rising bourgeoisie] in decaying feudal society." This is an important point. It shows that Marx's theory of social change, which is expressed in the tension between "productive forces" and "property relations," and which attempts to lay bare the mechanisms of internal, macrocosmic change, should not be treated as a closed system.

4. New markets rendered guild production inadequate.

Unlike capitalist "crises" which are crises of "overproduction," the crisis of the guild system was characterized by *under-production* caused by a technical basis inadequate for the satisfaction of the new markets.

5. Guild production was replaced by division of labor in manufacture resting on a similar but more efficient technical basis.

6. The unceasing expansion of markets and rising demand rendered even manufacture inadequate. Industrial production was revolutionized by steam and machinery. Manufacture was replaced by modern large-scale industry.

7. The modern bourgeoisie is therefore the product of a long process of development, of a series of revolutions in the "mode of production" and the means of communication.

8. "Each step in the development of the bourgeoisie was accompanied by a corresponding political advance."

The bourgeoisie, a subordinate class in the feudal system, grew in power until it finally achieved political hegemony in the modern representative state.

9. "The modern state authority is nothing more than a committee for the administration of the consolidated affairs of the bourgeois class as a whole."

10. "The bourgeoisie has played an extremely revolutionary role upon the stage of history."

Essentially this role was expressed in two processes: (a) tearing "asunder the motley feudal ties that bound men to their 'natural superiors';" and (b) creating and revolutionizing the capitalist mode of production.

11. Under the capitalist system the doctor, lawyer, priest, poet, and scientist—in short, professionals of all kinds, who were previously regarded with awe, have become wage-laborers.

12. "Urged onward by the need for an ever-expanding market, the bourgeoisie invades every quarter of the globe. It occupies every corner; forms settlements and sets up means of communication here, there, and everywhere."

13. As a consequence of this invasion, native industries are

destroyed, the corresponding social relations are changed, and new wants appear which can be satisfied by capitalist industry only.

14. Local and national self-sufficiency, and relative isolation, are replaced by an international system of intercourse. The interdependence of nations becomes the rule.

15. These changes affect intellectual as well as material products. Particularism and traditionalism become increasingly impossible.

16. More advanced capitalist countries force less developed nations to adopt capitalist methods of production.

17. The bourgeoisie subjects the countryside to the rule of the town.

18. Industrial concentration and centralization have laid the groundwork for political centralization. "Independent or loosely federated provinces, with disparate interests, laws, governments, and customs tariffs, have been consolidated into a single nation, with one government, one code of laws, one national class interest . . . ."

19. Just as previously capitalist productive forces came in conflict with feudal property relations, so now modern forces of production come in conflict with capitalist property relations.

Major manifestations of this tendency are the recurrent crises of the capitalist system which portend the breakdown of the system. These crises lead not only to the destruction of large quantities of finished products, they lead as well to the partial destruction of the existing forces of production.

20. Work has been divested of its individual character by machinery and modern industry and has consequently lost all charm for the workers. The worker has become a mere appendage to the machine.

21. As modern industry develops the work of men is increasingly displaced by the work of women and children.

22. All older classes and intermediate strata are slowly eliminated by modern industry. Small manufacturers and small traders, craftsmen and peasants, all fall into the ranks of the proletariat.

23. The workers pass through various stages of development in their struggle with the bourgeoisie.

At first they fight individually; then those in a single factory make common cause; later the workers of one trade combine throughout a whole locality. The unity which the workers achieve at first is not the outcome of their own inclination, "but is a consequence of the union of the bourgeoisie, which, for its own political purposes, must set the whole proletariat in motion, and can still do so at times." More and more the conflicts between workers and capitalists take on the character of a struggle between classes. Increasingly the working class becomes aware of its interests until it is transformed from a "class-in-itself" to a "class-for-itself." Although this tendency is counteracted by competition among the workers themselves, their unity is continually reformed and becomes stronger until they organize to form a class, i.e., to form a political party of their own.

24. The advance of industry precipitates whole sections of the ruling class into the proletariat. Parts of the ruling class, and especially some of the bourgeois intellectuals who have achieved a theoretical understanding of the historical movement as a whole, join the proletariat.

25. "Among all the classes that confront the bourgeoisie today, the proletariat alone is really revolutionary. Other classes decay and perish with the rise of large-scale industry, but the proletariat is the most characteristic product of that industry."

26. The members of the *lumpenproletariat,* thrown off by the lowest strata of society, i.e., the chronically unemployed, demoralized, and criminal elements of society, tend to become the "venal tools of the forces of reaction."

27. "The progress of industry, which the bourgeoisie involuntarily and passively promotes, substitutes for the isolation of the workers by mutual competition their revolutionary unification by association . . . . Before all, therefore, the bourgeoisie produces its own grave diggers. Its downfall and the victory of the proletariat are equally inevitable."

28. "The proletariat will use its political supremacy in order, by degrees, to wrest all capital from the bourgeoisie, to centralize all the means of production into the hands of the state (this meaning the proletariat organized as ruling class), and, as rapidly as possible, to increase the total mass of productive forces."

29. When the proletariat makes itself the ruling class, "and as such forcibly sweeps away the old system of production—it there-

with sweeps away the system upon which class conflicts depend, makes an end of classes and thus abolishes its own rule as a class."

30. "The old bourgeois society, with its classes and class conflicts, will be replaced by an association in which the free development of each will lead to the free development of all." The abolition of classes and class-conflict, Marx believed, would also lead to the disappearance of *the state;* for this institution, being a creature of class society, would have no function to perform in a classless civilization.

THE STATE

For Marx and Engels, the state is a special institutionalized public force "which is no longer immediately identical with the people's own organization of themselves as an armed power." [12] This institution had not always existed, they believed, nor was it evident in every society of their time. To be sure, even the "primitive communal" societies, which Engels discussed in his well-known book on the origin of the state, had some kind of public power which certain men held at certain times for specific purposes. But this power was firmly rooted in the people as a whole so that usurpation of power by separate individuals or groups or the perpetuation of such power against the will of the people was quite unthinkable. Basing himself on the work of Lewis Henry Morgan and other 19th-century anthropologists, Engels described the social condition in which the state was an unknown institution but in which a certain amount of authority was nonetheless delegated to certain members of the society.

The people elected or installed their war-chiefs and other leaders and also had the right to depose them. A tribal council composed of these leaders—whose powers were severely limited to specific occasions and periods—"held its deliberations in public, surrounded by the other members of the tribe, who had the right to join freely in the discussion and to make their views heard. The decision rested with the council. As a rule, everyone was given a hearing who asked for it; the women could also have their views expressed by a speaker of their own choice. Among the Iroquois the final decision had to be unanimous, as was also the case in regard to many decisions of the German mark communities." [13] This organization of authority settled all the disputes which arose within the society and also attended to the conflicts with other tribes. The political organization of society corresponded to the prevailing economic and other social conditions. The population is extremely sparse, and "the division of labor is purely primitive, between the sexes only. The man fights in the wars, goes hunting and fishing, procures the raw materials of food and tools necessary for doing so. The woman looks after the home and the preparation of food and clothing, cooks, weaves, sews. They are each master in their own sphere: the man in the forest, the woman in the house. Each is owner of the instruments which he or she makes or uses: the man of the weapons, the hunting and fishing implements, the woman of the household gear . . . . What is made and used in common is common property—the house, the garden, the long-boat." [14] Here was a society in which there was no private property in land and other productive resources to which some had rights of access and others did not; there were no rich or poor, no rulers or ruled.

When the state finally does appear in certain societies (Engels reviews this development among the Athenians, the Romans, the Celts and the Germans) it is not a force imposed from without; nor is it as in Hegel the realization of Reason or the Idea. Rather, it is a product of social development at a certain stage and emerges together with private property in the means of production, the crystallization of classes, and class-conflict. Private property and inequalities in wealth give rise to social stratification and class cleavages thus undermining the solidarity of the society as a whole. The state, then, "is the admission that this society has involved itself in insoluble self-contradiction and is cleft into irreconcilable antagonism which it is powerless to exorcize. But in order that these antagonisms, classes with conflicting economic interests, shall not consume themselves and society in fruitless struggle, a power, apparently standing above society, had become necessary to moderate the conflict and keep it within the bounds of 'order'; and this power, arisen out of society, but placing itself above it and increasingly alienating itself from it, is the state." [15]

Class-conflict has undermined the unity of society and the state is now necessary as a coercive instrument. The means of violence now come under the control of a special group which if it is not the propertied class itself is nonetheless ultimately under the control of that class. The state and all its institutions serve the function of holding in check the propertyless masses. And this applies equally to the slaves of ancient civilization, the serfs under feudalism, and the wage-earners under capitalism. In all class societies, instruments of political power are created to safeguard the economic power of the propertied.

The coercive and repressive function of the state becomes more prominent the more the intensity of class-conflict increases and the greater the danger of revolution.

"This public force exists in every state; it consists not merely of armed men, but also of material appendages, prisons, and coercive institutions of all kinds, of which [primitive] society knew nothing. It may be very insignificant, practically negligible, in societies with still undeveloped class antagonisms . . . as at times and in places in the United States of America. But it becomes stronger in proportion as the class antagonisms within the state become sharper and as adjoining states grow larger and more populous. It is enough to look at Europe today, where class-struggle and rivalry in conquest have brought the public power to a pitch that it threatens to devour the whole of society. . . ." [16] Here, as we see, although Engels mentions national rivalry as contributing to the maintenance and growth of the coercive instruments of the state, he treats this as a less important factor than class-conflict within the society. The state does not stand "above" the classes to mediate between them but rather serves to ensure the continued domination of the economically most powerful class. This is true in a democratic republic as well "which in our modern social conditions become more and more an unavoidable necessity and is the form of state in which alone the last decisive battle between proletariat and bourgeoisie can be fought out—the democratic republic no longer officially recognizes differences of property. Wealth here employs its power indirectly, but all the more surely. It does this in two ways: by plain corruption of officials, of which America is the classic example, and by an alliance between the government and the stock exchange . . . ." [17]

To summarize, the state emerged under specific economic and social circumstances which resulted in the cleavage of society into classes. The state was therefore necessary so long as that cleavage continued to exist. If classes and hence class-conflict could be eliminated from society, then the state would lose its *raison d'être*. This was not a vision of a far-off future but a real possibility. "We are now rapidly approaching a stage in the development of production at which the existence of these classes has not only ceased to be a necessity, but becomes a positive hindrance to production. They will fall as inevitably as they once arose. The state inevitably falls with them. The society which organizes production anew on the basis of free and equal association of the producers will put the whole state machinery where it will then belong—into the museum of antiquities, next to the spinning wheel and the bronze ax." [17] The process by which this was actually to come about became clearer—so Marx and Engels believed—only after the publication of the *Manifesto*.

From the time of the appearance of the *Manifesto* to the failure of the Paris Commune, more than 20 years elapsed. The experience of the intervening years demonstrated to Marx and Engels that in some respects the principles laid down in 1848 had to be amended and revised. In 1872, when they jointly republished the *Communist Manifesto*, they remarked in the preface to the German edition that while its general principles were on the whole as correct then as before, nevertheless "the practical application of the principles will depend, as the *Manifesto* itself states, everywhere and at all times, on the historical conditions for the time being existing." [18] One revision, however, was absolutely essential in the light of three developments: (a) the immense industrial growth since the *Manifesto* first appeared; (b) the experience of the revolutions in France and Germany in 1848, and finally, (c) the experience of the Paris Commune in 1871. Referring to his work *The Civil War in France*, written after the Commune, Marx stated the revision thus: ". . . the working class cannot simply lay hold of the ready-made state machinery, and wield it for its own purposes." [19] Marx had somewhat anticipated this conclusion in his articles on the *18th Brumaire of Louis Bonaparte*. In a letter to Kugelmann on April 12, 1871, written during the Commune, Marx explained the point of view he had arrived at some 20 years before. "If you look at the last chapter of my Eighteenth Brumaire, you will find that I say that the next attempt of the French Revolution will be no longer as before, to transfer the bureaucratic-military machine from one hand to another, but to *smash* it, and this is the preliminary condition for every real people's revolution *on the continent*." [20] The phrase "on the continent," has been underscored to emphasize the fact that Marx explicitly specified the conditions to which his propositions applied. Heavy fighting or violence was required not by every revolution but only those taking place where state-bureaucracies were highly developed. In this connection, it is known that Marx, as late as 1872, remarked that "the workers may hope to secure their ends by peaceful means" in countries like Great Britain, the United States, and Holland. [21]

In all revolutions, however, Marx was confident that the taking of power by the working class would involve a period of transition marked by the *dictatorship of the proletariat*. Although this concept can be logically inferred from the *Manifesto,* the phrase *dictatorship of the proletariat* was explicitly employed for the first time by Marx in a letter to Weydemeyer written in 1852. In that letter Marx wrote: "What I did that was new was to prove: . . . that the class struggle necessarily leads to the *dictatorship of the proletariat;* . . . ." [22] No concept employed by Marx has been the subject of as much misinterpretation as this one.

Marx provided some clarification the second time he employed the concept in his *Critique of the Gotha Program,* written in 1875. Describing the transition period between capitalism and socialism, Marx wrote: "Between capitalist and communist society lies the period of the revolutionary transformation of the one into the other. There corresponds to this also a political transition period in which the state can be nothing but the *revolutionary dictatorship of the proletariat*." [23] Before the Paris Commune, however, there was no concrete historical event which could be pointed to as an example of working-class dictatorship. The Commune provided just such an event. On the 20th anniversary of the Commune, in 1891, Engels wrote in his introduction to the *Civil War in France:* ". . . do you want to know what this dictatorship looks like? Look at the Paris Commune. That was the *Dictatorship of the Proletariat*." [24]

From Engel's identification of the Commune with proletarian

dictatorship, it becomes clear what was and was not meant by this phrase. The Commune was based on the support of the majority as determined by universal suffrage. The acceptance of the people's right to frequent elections of their representatives implies full popular participation in the working of the "dictatorship." The Commune was exercised through the elected body based upon popular choice and subject to public opinion. Public opinion prevailed through the institution of recall, i.e., the right to depose any representative chosen. Marx's praise of the workings of the Commune shows beyond any doubt that nothing could be more foreign to his view than the supersession of universal suffrage by the rule of a party. It seems inescapable that Marx and Engels did not equate the dictatorship of the proletariat with the dictatorship of a party over the rest of the community. They are explicit on this score: "The Communists do not form a separate party opposed to other working-class parties. They have no interests separate and apart from the proletariat as a whole." [25]

From the foregoing discussion, then, this much seems to be clear. From Marx's standpoint, class-conflict was leading to a revolution and to a dictatorship of the proletariat, a transitory but democratic phase in which repression of class enemies may be a necessity. In some places, notably on the continent, the bureaucratic mechanism could not be simply laid hold of, but had to be smashed. In other places, such as England, a parliamentary transition from capitalism to socialism was *possible*. In all places the working-class dictatorship was to lead to a "withering away" of the state. This is a logical inference from the *Manifesto* as well as from Marx's explicit praise of the Communards who considered their rule temporary. Their incumbency, based on the will of the people, was itself a transition stage during which their power would become increasingly unnecessary. Consequently, their power would be relinquished slowly and the rule by men over men would be replaced by the administration of things.

CRITICAL EVALUATION OF MARX'S MAJOR
THEORETICAL PROPOSITIONS

In this section Marx's major theoretical propositions are critically discussed. The propositions are first succinctly stated and then followed by critical remarks.

1. The totality of the relations of production constitutes the most important sphere of a society and its economic foundation. The economic foundation determines the character of the society as a whole as well as the psychology of the people within it.

2. The social change which a society as a whole undergoes is a function of the tension between developing forces of production and existing property relations.

3. Class-conflict between capitalists and workers is an expression in the economic, political, and other spheres, of the objective conflict of interests between the two classes.

The discussion of Marx's conception of the capitalist mode of production, and the analysis of "productive forces" and "relations of production" have made amply clear the precise meaning which Marx assigned to these concepts. A criticism has often been raised, however, pointing to the inadequacy of the concepts as clearly separated operational definitions. C. Wright Mills, for example, has argued that the "institutional organization of a society, including relations of production, certainly penetrate deeply into technological implements and their scientific developments, including forces of production, shaping their meaning and their role in historical change. Many factors that cannot clearly be considered 'economic' enter into what Marx seems to mean by 'mode of production' or 'economic base.'" [26] This "interpenetration of spheres" which Mills observed was acknowledged earlier in this study when it was stated that the productive potential of a society cannot be measured apart from its property relations. This does not mean, however, that the various institutional orders of a society cannot be delineated.

Certainly in advanced industrial societies today the economic, political and military orders are distinguishable as separate orders despite their interdependence. That Marx himself recognized the interpenetration of spheres is clear from his adoption of the term *political economy* to describe the focus of his studies. However, this did not prevent him from distinguishing the various orders in society nor from assigning causal weight to each. On the theoretical level, the important point for Marx is that one sphere of social conduct has "causal priority" in effecting changes in other spheres; and here Marx may have been right, for he had observed the many social changes that followed on the heels of the Industrial Revolution. On the methodological level, the main point is that to understand the various spheres of the superstructure, they should not be studied as autonomous developments since they do not change or develop autonomously. In the language of the sociology of knowledge, these spheres should be studied not in *immanent* terms but in terms of their *transcendent* development. It can be granted in this regard that the terms "foundation" and "superstructure" may be an unfortunate choice of terms. But if we think of spheres of social conduct, or institutional orders, then the relationship which Marx imputed to the economic foundation and its superstructure becomes much clearer.

In these propositions, however, Marx is most vague where we would require him to be the clearest. As some students of Marx have observed, the problem of mediation, i.e., precisely *how* the foundation determines the superstructure, is not well worked out. Engels recognized this as a conspicuous omission from his and Marx's work and expressly acknowledged it in a letter to Franz Mehring: ". . . one more point is lacking, which, Marx and I always failed to stress enough in our writings and in regard to which we are all equally guilty. That is to say, we all laid, and *were bound* to lay, the main emphasis, in the first place, on the *derivation* of political, juridical and other ideological notions, and of actions arising through the medium of these notions, from basic economic facts. But in so doing we neglected the formal side—the ways and means by which these notions, etc., come about—for the sake of the content." [27]

This problem is considered, in part, in the following chapter. For now it will suffice to make the following observations. It will be noted in the third proposition that for Marx class conflict is an expression in various spheres of the objective conflict of interests existing between the two classes. Class conflict, particularly on the political level, is predicated on the assumption of growing class-consciousness on the part of the workers. How does proletarian existence lead to proletarian consciousness? How do the workers, according to Marx, gain this awareness and transform themselves into a class-for-itself? Marx offers at least three possibilities: The workers will gain this awareness (a) spontaneously, as a result of their own experience; (b) they will gain it from declassed bourgeois elements who join their ranks; and (c) from intellectuals who have achieved a theoretical understanding of the historical movement as a whole.

As an over-all evaluation of these propositions, the following observations may be made. Marx's economic determinism was and continues to be a fruitful *hypothesis* in the study of macrodynamics, or the mode of change of a society as a whole. This in spite of the fact that it was intended by Marx as a *historically specific theory* relating to the period of the origin and development of capitalism in western Europe and not to societies in general, irrespective of time and place. For Marx these propositions were neither a historical-philosophical theory nor a supra-historical construct to be applied *a priori* to every society and every period. Marx vehemently dissociated himself from the attempt to transform his emphasis, which was accurate under certain historical circumstances, into a universal historical principle. In a letter to Mikhailovsky, he rejected the latter's attempt to transform his sketch of the origins of capitalism in western Europe into a historical-philosophical theory "of the general path every people is fated to tread, whatever the historical circumstances in which it finds itself . . . . But I beg his pardon. (He is both honoring and shaming me too much.)" [28] Similarly, in another letter, in which he clarified what he meant by "historical inevitability," Marx wrote: "Hence the 'historical inevitability' of this movement [the genesis of capitalism] is *expressly* limited to the *countries of Western Europe*." [29] Thus Marx's propositions which attach causal priority to the economic foundation were based upon the empirical-historical evidence of a specific epoch in the history of western Europe.

That Marx intended this proposition—on the determining influence of the economic order—to be understood as a historically specific one is supported not only by his own statements to that effect but also, for example, by Max Weber's interpretation of it. Weber interpreted Marx's proposition as one arrived at after studying developments in western Europe during a definite period and therefore undertook to "test" its validity not just "anywhere" but in the same historical context. In effect, Weber was continuing the discussion of Marx's theoretical work which was begun by scholars of the German Historical School, particularly Toennies and Sombart.[30] They were much concerned with introducing a "corrective" factor into the Marxian hypothesis and actually their criticism was aimed not so much at Marx's work as toward that of his followers (whose vulgarization of his ideas Marx recognized and severely rebuked). Continuing the line of inquiry begun by the German school, Weber argued that the problem of the psychological foundations of capitalism has been ignored; insufficient attention has been paid to the psychological conditions which made the development of capitalism possible. Marx's own discussions suggested that the "spirit of capitalism" was pretty much a product of the developing capitalist mode of production. Weber argued that one might profitably look elsewhere for the source of the ethos which was so congruent with the capitalistic spirit and which perhaps even antedated that complex system of institutions called capitalism.

Weber agreed with Marx that capitalism was a modern phenomenon. It was modern in that it rested on rationally organized productive enterprise, legally free wage earners, and the reinvestment of profits for the expansion of capital. This kind of capitalism was quite different from previous forms of "capitalistic" activity such as speculation, money-lending, commerce, piracy, etc., which probably were as old as history. The problem which intrigued Weber was how this modern system—involving a code of economic conduct and system of social relations sharply at variance with established traditions and conventions and with the law of church and state—established itself. The new system could not be considered either "natural" or "inevitable." As R. H. Tawney has observed: "So questionable an innovation demanded of the pioneers who first experimented with it as much originality, self-confidence, and tenacity of purpose as is required to-day of those who would break from the net that it has woven. What influence moved them to defy tradition? From what source did they derive the principles to replace it?" [31] To answer these questions Weber undertook his prodigious project which has left us voluminous studies not only of European developments but of ancient China, India, and Israel as well. His last pronouncements on the subject can be found in his *General Economic History*.[32]

With fastidious care he traces the development of the various institutions which culminated in the modern economic system and finally takes up the problem of the evolution of the capitalistic spirit. One by one he considers the many variables which were alleged to be the key factors in the appearance of capitalism—population growth, influx of precious metals, geographic conditions, rational enterprise, etc.

From the beginning of the 18th to the end of the 19th centuries, in the west as well as in China, the population grew to an approximately equal extent; in spite of this fact capitalism was not advanced in China. A population of a minimum size is a necessary but not sufficient condition for the advancement of capitalism, argues Weber. Likewise with Sombart's thesis about the importance of precious metals in the appearance of capitalism. Other societies at other times also amassed enormous quantities of precious metals; these, however, far from being directed to rational enterprise, were squandered. In India, for example, "the greater part of the precious metals disappeared in the hands of the rajahs instead of being converted into cash and applied in the establishment of enterprises of a rational capitalistic character. This fact proves that it depends entirely upon the nature of the labor system what tendency will result from an inflow of precious metal." [33]

Geographical conditions were also important. To be sure, argues Weber, inland commerce on the vast land masses of China and India was extremely expensive owing to the enormous costs of transportation and this ". . . formed serious obstructions for the classes who were in a position to make profits through trade and to use trading capital in the construction of a capitalistic system, while in the west the position of the Mediterranean as an inland sea, and the abundant interconnections through the rivers, favored the opposite development of international commerce." [34] Here again, however, these conditions must not be overestimated because "capitalism in the west was born in the industrial cities of the interior, not in the cities which were centers of sea trade." [35] After considering many other developments, including the various manifestations of rationality in the modern economic system, e.g., rational accounting, rational technology, and rational law, Weber concludes that these too—despite his opinion that they produced capitalism in the last resort—were not the sole factors. "Necessary complementary factors were the rational spirit, the rationalization of the conduct of life in general, and a rationalistic economic ethic." [36] For Weber this spirit or ethic was the result of move-

ments which originated in the religious revolution of the 16th
century.

In his essay on the Protestant ethic, Weber traced this spirit to
the ethical injunctions of ascetic Protestantism. Fully recognizing
the role of the economic and other developments, he was in this
instance centering his attention on the role of religion. In no
sense was he arguing a psychological determinism of capitalist
development. Once, while replying to a critic of his essay who
charged him with taking an idealistic position, Weber admitted
that unfortunately it was possible to construe his thesis in this way
owing to certain turns of phrase. He therefore promised that in
subsequent revisions of the essay he would remove all formulations
which suggest the derivation of institutions from religious mo-
tives.[37] In addition, it is clear that Weber felt that in his essays on
religion he had completed only half the task he set himself. For
in order that the problem of the rise of capitalism be given the attention it deserved, he believed it was necessary to trace influences
in a direction opposite to that in his essay. Never carrying out this
project, he once remarked ironically that had he done so ". . . he
would probably have been accused of having capitulated to historical materialism, even as he was now charged with an overemphasis
on the religious or ideological factor." [38]

How has Weber's thesis, as a critical corrective to Marx's emphasis, stood up under the attack of its own critics? They have
raised at least three important objections to Weber's thesis. The
first is a matter of historical fact and was raised by the German
scholar, Lujo Brentano. Brentano in his *Anfange des Kapitalismus*
argued that Weber attributed to Protestantism many developments
which were present during the Renaissance; and R. H. Tawney
and other contemporary scholars tend to agree that "Brentano's
criticism, that the political thought of the Renaissance was as
powerful a solvent of conventional restraints as the teaching of
Calvin, is not without weight." [39] Tawney goes on to make an observation that would seem to justify the absence on Marx's part, of
any special attention to the role of religion in the origin of the
capitalist system. Tawney writes that "In England, at any rate, the
speculations of business men and economists as to money, prices,
and the foreign exchanges, which were occasioned by the recurrent
financial crises of the sixteenth century and by the change in the

price level, were equally effective in undermining the attitude which Weber called traditionalism." [40]

A second objection to Weber's thesis is that the values he attributed almost exclusively to Calvinism were part of a more general intellectual movement and that these values were "reflected in the outlook of Catholic, as well as Protestant, writers." [41]

Finally, there is the criticism raised by Tawney himself. He points out that Weber's illustrations of his thesis are drawn primarily from the writings of English Puritans of the late 17th century. In this way Weber presents religious opinions on economic ethics which had themselves been influenced by changes in economic life. Tawney writes: "For three generations of economic development and political agitation lay between these writers and the author of the *Institutes*. The Calvinism which fought the English Civil War, still more the Calvinism which won an uneasy toleration at the Revolution, was not that of its founder." [42] In his major work on this subject Tawney writes: "To think of the abdication of religion from its theoretical primacy over economic activity and social institutions as synchronizing with the revolt from Rome, is to antedate a movement which was not finally accomplished for another century and a half, and which owed as much to changes in economic and political organization, as it did to developments in the sphere of religious thought." [43] Thus Weber, by choosing illustrations not from the early phase of iron collectivism under Calvin but from the second individual phase which crystallized 100 or 150 years later, neglected to examine the extent to which religious opinions were themselves effects of the changing economic and political organization. Had Weber carried out his plan to trace influences in the opposite direction—the economic and political upon the religious—it would be clearer than it is even now that his work was not intended, nor should it be regarded, as a refutation of Marx's hypothesis.

Right or wrong, however, Weber's thesis remains important because it alerts students of society to problems which Marx, because of the focus of his interests, neglected. When generalized, Weber's thesis states in effect that there are attitudinal prerequisites of industrialization and modernization and that these psychological conditions, as well as "relations of production," may either impede or facilitate, accelerate or retard, industrial and other modernizing developments. Sensing the importance of this viewpoint, social scientists have fruitfully generalized Weber's thesis: It is not the thesis in its particularity that is important—i.e., the emphasis on ascetic Protestantism—but the assumption that a functionally equivalent configuration of attitudes is a necessary condition of modernization. In these terms, contemporary students have stressed that the degree to which appropriate attitudes are present or absent is extremely important for the process of industrialization in particular and modernization in general. Moreover, while Weber was interested in such attitudes primarily among the members of one stratum—the pioneering industrialists, the entrepreneurs—contemporary students have studied other strata of the population, particularly the labor force. Given the desire for industrialization on the part of elites and certain strata of underdeveloped areas, "labor supply" cannot be taken for granted and is not a simple problem. A distinguished student of modernization has stated the problem this way:

> In the studies and theories of economic development, the subtler aspects of labor supply have been largely neglected. This neglect has arisen in part from an exclusively quantitative, demographic approach to manpower or "labor force," in part from a naive view of economic motivation . . . . The problem of labor supply in its full social and psychological significance, is, therefore, the core of our inquiry. Specifically, what are the cultural, institutional, sociopsychological factors that induce or impede the transition from nonindustrial to industrial employment? [44]

To preclude any misunderstanding of his approach, Wilbert E. Moore writes:

> It is not to be supposed that the problem so defined implicitly denies the relevance of the more commonly understood "economic" elements in industrial development: natural resources and their topographical accessibility, markets and transportation, capital accumulation, and the appropriate forms of organization and direction. Rather it is assumed that these factors constitute necessary but not sufficient conditions and leave out of account the possible cultural impediments to their use.[45]

It is clear, then, that both emphases—those inspired by Marx *and* Weber—are important and, moreover, that they complement each other. It is for this reason that Weber's work should be viewed not in opposition to Marx but as an effort to round out the latter's method.[46]

Since Marx's time it has become increasingly evident that the exclusive emphasis on the economic foundation, in effecting changes in the other institutional orders of society, is inadequate. The changes in the structure of capitalism during the 20th century have pointed up the determining character of the political and even the military orders. This means that since Marx's time the political order, for example, may have acquired greater autonomy and can, under certain conditions, determine the economic system of a society. To conclude, all "determinisms," whether economic, political, military, or religious, would have been considered by Marx not as dogmatic principles but as hypotheses, subject to test.

4. Ownership or non-ownership of the means of production is the objective criterion of class membership. The owners and the workers are the two basic classes of the capitalist system.

There are two reasons for Marx's selection of this criterion. In part it is due to his method of abstraction in *Capital* and in part to his expectations about the development of the capitalist system. This method, the two-class model, was dictated by the problem he set himself, i.e., laying bare the "laws of motion," the dynamics of the system. His focus on only two classes was required by his model and must not be taken to mean that he ignored other classes or regarded them as unimportant. Later, in our examination of his journalistic writings, it will be seen that far from ignoring other classes, he analyzed them into their minute strata.

However, if Marx's focus on two classes is a function of his model, it is also due to his expectations about capitalist development. There can be little doubt that as he projected the trends of the capitalist system, its continuous development was supposed to eliminate, slowly but surely, all older and intermediate classes and strata and leave basically two classes. In part, this tendency has prevailed. The development of large-scale industry under capitalism has drastically decreased the proportion of small producers, small capitalists, and small shopkeepers. In his study of the "old" and "new" middle classes in the United States, for example, C. Wright Mills wrote that: "The free entrepreneurs of the old middle classes have diminished as a proportion of the gainfully occupied. They no longer enjoy the social position they once held. They no longer are models of aspiration for the population at large. They no longer fulfill their classic role as integrators of the social structure in which they live and work. These are the indices of their decline. The causes of that decline involve the whole push and shove of modern industrial society." [47] More recently this trend was summarized in similar terms: "In brief, then, small businesses are producing less return on their investments than are large businesses. Their total number is showing a relative decline, in that the American business population is growing at a slower rate than either the general population of the country or our gross national product. Many firms continue to disappear because of mergers or other acquisitions by large businesses, increasing the concentration of economic power in the hands of larger concerns." [48] Although Marx partially foresaw this tendency, he did not foresee the displacement of this class by the phenomenal growth of the new middle class.

Can ownership or non-ownership of means of production, as a criterion of class, be regarded as a fruitful analytical tool? The study of social stratification has shown that it is indispensable for an understanding of structured inequality in any society. Taken alone, however, it is, as Mills has indicated, "inadequate and misleading, even for understanding economic stratification." [49] Property as a criterion must be supplemented by income, its source and its size, the position one occupies in the economic structure, and the authority and prestige it imparts. Certainly prestige and related phenomena impinging on and determining the self-image of an individual can neither be explained nor understood on the basis of property alone. This is true of class-consciousness and political awareness too. Mills has observed that: "In capitalist societies, among the immense majority who are propertyless, distinctions of status and occupation lead to or away from just those psychological and political consequences of economic stratification expected by Marx." [50] For example, the white-collar employees share with production or factory workers common relations of production; both are non-owners. Following Marx's logic, since their objective conditions are similar their psychological approach should also be similar, which is clearly not so. Such an approach would therefore yield little, for to treat them together as one class would throw little light on one of the most consequential developments in advanced capitalist countries.

Some social scientists have attempted to salvage Marx's two-class model by generalizing it to include political power. Property may have been the basis of power under Victorian capitalism but this is not as true of 20th century capitalism. Now power and authority flow from the relative position one occupies in an "imperatively coordinated association." According to Dahrendorf, for example, Marx's two-class model can be useful not necessarily by applying it to society as a whole but to separate associations. Thus the dichotomous view of power is retained since in every association a superordinate and subordinate stratum can be observed. Moreover, according to Dahrendorf's view, the conflicting classes even as Marx saw them do exist, if not in society as a whole then at least, in the sphere of industry. In Dahrendorf's words:

> In the sphere of industry we encounter the conflicting classes in full formation. In a way, the conditions of industry in post-capitalist society might be described as an empirical analogue of the model of class theory, an ideal type come true. The authority structure of the enterprise generates the two quasi-groups of management and labor, along with their latent interests; from these are recruited the interest groups of employers' associations and trade unions, with their specific manifest interests. For many decades, now, the disputes between trade unions and employers' associations have presented the well-known picture of industrial conflict.[51]

Thus Marx's two-class model is not entirely useless. What about his prediction of the growing dichotomization of power? Later, it will be seen that the dichotomization which Marx predicted is indeed taking place, but in a different form from which he expected.

5. Class-conflict is a normal and unavoidable condition in capitalist society.

Marx did not discover class conflict nor did he offer this idea as a dogmatic *a priori* construct. As he himself stated, ". . . no credit is due me for discovering the existence of classes in modern society, nor yet the struggle between them. Long before me bourgeois historians had described the historical development of this struggle of the classes and bourgeois economists the economic anatomy of the classes." [52] From this angle, Marx was merely reasserting what he believed to be an established fact. Of course, the fact of class conflict received special emphasis in his hands just as before and after him the "harmonistic" view has received emphasis in the hands of many social thinkers. One could argue, as has Schumpeter, that in social life "antagonism and synagogism are of course both ubiquitous and in fact inseparable except in the rarest of cases." [53] But in describing the basic relationship of the two classes under capitalism it is an exaggeration to argue, as some have, that the true interests of management and labor are one and the same.[54] If this were so, how could even the minor conflicts between them, e.g., strikes, be explained?

Marx's conclusion as to the normalcy of class conflict was an empirical-historical proposition and not, as some have insisted, an *a priori* construct. Schumpeter, for example, believing that it was a construct dictated by the goal Marx imputed to the history of the capitalist system, wrote that if "class struggle was the subject matter of history and also the means of bringing about the socialist dawn, and *if* there had to be just those two classes, then their relation had to be antagonistic in principle or else the force in his system of social dynamics would have been lost." [55] Here Schumpeter is treating Marx as a Hegelian and ignoring the empirical basis for Marx's generalization. This, as we shall try to show, is an untenable interpretation of Marx's conception of class conflict.

What did Marx mean by class struggle? There can be no doubt that for Marx the term covered a variety of phenomena and that "struggle" could take many forms. At one extreme it clearly included struggle by force of arms and open physical combat between the working class and its opponents. In *Class Struggles in France, 1848-1850,* referring to the February days of the struggles of 1848, Marx wrote: "But the workers were determined this time not to put up with any bamboozlement like that of July 1830. They were ready to take up the fight anew and get a republic by force of arms." [56] And further on, referring to the June days of the same struggles, he wrote: "The workers were left no choice; they had to starve or let fly. They answered on June 22 with the tremendous insurrection in which the first great battle was fought between the two classes that split modern society. It was a fight for the preservation or annihilation of the bourgeois order . . . ." [57] Marx went on to describe how the workers held in check for five days the army, the Mobile Guard, the Paris National Guard, and the National Guard that streamed in from the provinces. Thus in some places, notably on the continent, and under certain circumstances, the conflict of interests between the classes could and did take the form of violent and bloody struggles. Even in the 20th century, and in countries where Marx envisioned a peaceful transition to socialism, violence of a high degree accompanied class conflict. It is obvious, however, that struggles of such ferocity and intensity were not the rule but the exception.

Equally regarded as class struggle was that taking place in a parliamentary setting. Marx clearly regarded the debates by the political representative and ideological spokesmen of the two classes—*to the extent that these debates had concrete effects for the life-conditions of the classes*—as a form of class conflict. Here the underscored phrase is an important qualifying one. Whether the goings-on in parliament were to be taken seriously and considered consequential was for Marx an empirical question. In some cases, as in Germany during the struggles of 1848, Marx considered the parliament an impotent body and the proceedings in its midst a farce. He attacked its course of action and described its members as afflicted by a malady which he called *parliamentary cretinism,* "a disorder which penetrates its unfortunate victims with the solemn conviction that the whole world, its history and future, are governed by a majority of votes in that particular representative body . . . ." [58]

This was Marx's appraisal of the parliament in Germany as an arena of "struggle." On the other hand, in England, factory acts and other legislation were not without their effects and were differently evaluated by Marx. He wrote: "What could possibly show better the character of the capitalist mode of production, than the necessity that exists for forcing upon it, by acts of parliament, the simplest appliances for maintaining cleanliness and health?" [59] Of course, even in England passing legislation and seeing to its enforcement were two different matters. And Marx observed the "hesitation, the repugnance, and the bad faith, with which it [parliament] lent itself to the task of carrying those measures into practice." [60]

The best evidence, however, that what goes on at the ballot box and in parliament could be considered class struggle comes from one of Engels' last pronouncements on the subject which, incidentally, lent support to the Revisionist position. In 1895, in his introduction to *Class Struggles in France,* Engels described the phenomenal growth of the Social-Democratic party since 1866, the year universal suffrage was introduced in Germany. So phenomenal was this growth that the state, the instrument of the ruling class, for Marx, countered with the anti-Socialist Law, to which the working class countered again. Engels wrote that under the pressure of that law, "without a press, without a legal organization and without the right of combination and assembly, rapid expansion really began: 1884, 550,000; 1887, 763,000; 1890, 1,427,000 votes. Thereupon *the hand of the state was paralyzed.* The anti-Socialist Law disappeared . . . ." [61] The workers of Germany had "supplied their comrades in all countries *with a new weapon, and one of the sharpest,* when they showed them how to make use of universal suffrage." [62] (Italics mine.) Clearly, then, for Marx and Engels the class struggle was waged not only over barricades but at the ballot-box and in parliament as well. So much for the 19th century. What about the 20th?

Early theorists of the American labor movement recognized that working-class struggles against employers were indeed taking place. These struggles, however, were directed not toward the seizure of power, but toward limited economic aims. Selig Perlman, for example, believed that the trade-union movement fought for a maximum control over the job and for a maximum number of jobs.[63] For Perlman, the entire struggle of American labor was directed toward the betterment of its position within the framework of the existing order and not, as its European counterpart alleged about itself, toward a change of the existing order. Later in the century, particularly after World War II, it became clear in all advanced capitalist societies that class conflict is a normal phenomenon, that it expresses itself in various forms, and that electioneering, and other political processes in democratic societies, can be viewed as an expression of democratic class struggle. Thus S. M. Lipset writes that:

> In every modern democracy conflict among different groups is expressed through political parties which basically represent a

"democratic translation of the class struggle." Even though many parties renounce the principle of class conflict or loyalty, an analysis of their appeal and their support suggests that they do represent the interests of different classes. On a world scale, the principal generalization which can be made is that parties are primarily based on either the lower classes or the middle and upper classes." [64]

In developing his thesis, Lipset writes more explicitly that: "More than anything else the party struggle is a conflict among classes, and the most impressive single fact about political party support is that in virtually every economically developed country the lower income groups vote mainly for parties of the left, while the higher income groups vote mainly for parties of the right." [65] What is perhaps most striking about this generalization is that it ". . . holds true for the American parties, which have traditionally been considered an exception to the class-cleavage pattern of Europe. The Democrats from the beginning of their history have drawn more support from the lower strata of the society, while the Federalist, Whig, and Republican parties have held the loyalties of the more privileged groups." [66]

Similarly, R. M. MacIver believes that party politics cannot be understood without studying parties in their relationship to upper and lower classes and the conflict of interests among them.

> The right is always the party sector associated with the interests of the upper or dominant classes, the left the sector expressive of the lower economic or social classes, and the center that of the middle classes. Historically this criterion seems acceptable. The conservative right has defended entrenched prerogatives, privileges and powers; the left has attacked them. The right has been more favorable to the aristocratic position, to the hierarchy of birth or of wealth; the left has fought for the equalization of advantage or of opportunity, for the claims of the less advantaged. Defense and attack have met, under democratic conditions, not in the name of class but in the name of principle; but the opposing principles have broadly corresponded to the interests of the different classes.[67]

Here it may be of interest to note that even Talcott Parsons, who has been criticized for neglecting problems of conflict in society, finds it useful to analyze American political history in terms of the conflict between left and right. In his discussion of the line of differentiation between the two parties, the Democratic and Republican, Parsons writes:

I would like to characterize this distinction as that between "right" and "left" in a sense appropriate to American conditions. The focus of the American right in this sense is the organization of the free-enterprise economy . . . . [It] is *politically* conservative because the economy is institutionalized on a private-enterprise basis in such a way that positive political action can readily be defined as threatening to interfere with the conditions of operation of this type of economy.[68]

On the other hand, the "left," according to Parsons, has been "The focus of those elements predisposed to favor positive action on the political level who have been favorable to 'reform' of various sorts, to control of the economy, to promotion of 'welfare,' and not least to 'interventionism' in foreign affairs." [69]

In addition to class conflict assuming a relatively peaceful and democratic form, it has become increasingly clear, in all advanced industrial countries, that the regulation and insulation of this conflict is possible. Some observers have described this as the transformation of class struggle into administrative regulation. Bargaining and regulation, however, are made possible precisely by the recognition on the part of the contending parties of their respective power positions.

What remains as true now as when Perlman studied the labor movement, is that "struggles" and bargaining procedures are directed toward limited economic aims. Insofar as unions represent the working class and labor-management controversy represents "class struggle," the object of the struggle is to receive a greater share of the social product and not the elimination of capitalism. C. Wright Mills has accordingly observed that under such conditions "class struggle in Marx's sense, or in any reasonable meaning that can be given to it, does not necessarily grow sharper, more open, more political in form." [70]

Any general conclusion about this proposition must acknowledge the prevalence of class conflict in a variety of forms. But it must equally acknowledge that it is an intermittent phenomenon, and that class-collaboration is also a fact of capitalist history.

6. Exploitation—the extraction of surplus-value from the labor of the worker—is an objective and unavoidable condition under capitalism.

For Marx exploitation describes an objective process and is

therefore not intended as a moral judgment. It would take us too far afield to enter the economic controversy about the relative validity of this theory. From a socio-political standpoint, however, the following may be observed:

(a) The capitalist system yields an enormous surplus-product over which its producers have little control. The control of this surplus, and power over its disposal, are in the hands—if not of a capitalist class—then of some kind of decision-making elite.

(b) To the extent that the above statement is true, the workers, having little or no control over the social product, would still have to be considered exploited. For Marx, control of the social product and of the means of production was to be acquired by the workers under socialism.

Of course, in no society, not even under socialism, could the working class appropriate the *total* social product. Marx recognized this and took great pains to point it out to working-class leaders who naively believed otherwise. In his *Critique of the Gotha Program,* he wrote:

> From this [the total social product] must now be deducted:
> *First,* cover for replacement of the means of production used up.
> *Secondly,* additional portion for expansion of production.
> *Thirdly,* reserve or insurance funds to provide against accidents, dislocations caused by natural calamities, etc. . . . .
> There remains the other part of the total product, intended to serve as means of consumption.
> Before this is divided among the individuals, there has to be deducted again, from it:
> *First, the general costs of administration not belonging to production.*
> This part will, from the outset, be very considerably restricted in comparison with present-day society and it diminishes in proportion as the new society develops.
> *Secondly, that which is intended for the common satisfaction of needs* such as schools, health service, etc.
> From the outset this part grows considerably in comparison with present-day society and it grows in proportion as the new society develops.
> *Thirdly, funds for those unable to work,* etc. . . .[71] (Italics in original.)

Hence, only after all these deductions have been made can the remainder be allocated for direct consumption by the individual producers of the cooperative society. For Marx, then, "exploitation" disappears in the new society not because the producers now directly consume the total social product but because the decision of what to produce and how to dispose of it is democratically made by them and not by an elite.

The conditions described above which may be regarded correctly or incorrectly as exploitation have not, as yet, heightened the probability for proletarian revolution in any advanced capitalist society.

7. A major tendency of the capitalist system is the polarization of its class structure into owners of the means of production, on the one hand, and workers, on the other.

The polarization and simplification of the class structure of capitalist society, as Marx predicted it, has not taken place. If anything, the opposite tendency has been the general one during the 20th century. With the advance of capitalism the stratification of its class structure has become more complex and diversified. Moreover, production workers have decreased as a proportion of the total work force and this trend will no doubt become more pronounced with automation.

In addition, the old middle classes have also dwindled and have been replaced by an enormous new middle class. Mills[72] and others have adequately described this phenomenon and it is too well known to be described again here. From Marx's standpoint the members of the new middle class could only be considered as part of the proletariat since they do not own the means of production. But it is clear that the white-collar employees do not regard themselves as such. Moreover, to treat them as "proletarians" would seriously limit our understanding of them. A more accurate classification would view the white-collar employees in the new 20th-century corporate context. Some insight could then be gained, perhaps, by classifying the higher echelon executives with the large property owners and viewing them as a superordinate group, the "corporate rich." In this scheme the middle and lower levels would constitute the subordinate group, thus retaining the semblance of a two-class model. But the latter levels cannot be understood merely as a new type of wage-earner. They do not fit the Marxian scheme and their phenomenal growth during the present century contradicts the prediction of a two-class polarization of modern capitalism.

8. The advance of capitalism will bring with it the growing impoverishment of the workers.

The interpretation of this proposition as a predictive one is widespread and offered by no less an authority than Joseph Schumpeter. Rendering Marx's German term *Verelendung* as "immiserization," Schumpeter wrote: "Marx undoubtedly held that in the course of capitalist evolution real wage rates and the standard of life of the masses would fall in the better-paid, and fail to improve in the worst-paid, strata and that this would come about not through any accidental or environmental circumstances but by virtue of the very logic of the capitalist process." [73] Schumpeter thus viewed Marx's proposition as a prediction and a singularly infelicitous one at that.

Other careful students of Marx, however, have argued that this proposition should be understood not as a prediction but as one tendency flowing from Marx's method of abstraction. Paul Sweezy, for example, believes that "the tendencies or laws enunciated in Volume I [of *Capital*] are not to be interpreted as direct predictions about the future. Their validity is relative to the level of abstraction on which they are derived and to the extent of the modifications which they must undergo when the analysis is brought to a more concrete level." [74] Sweezy goes on to say that the so-called law in question is derived on a high level of abstraction and that "it constitutes in no sense a concrete prediction about the future." [75]

George Lichtheim, another close student of Marx, concurs in this interpretation. Lichtheim states that Marx's proposition "cannot be described as a 'general law' of development. At most it represents an abstract tendency which asserts itself only in the absence of counteracting forces." [76] And again with respect to the same "law" Lichtheim writes:

> In actual fact pauperization plays no great part in the Marxian argument, apart from those passages where it is invoked to show what happens at the bottom of the social pyramid, where a "reserve army" of more or less permanently unemployed is "accumulated" by the mechanism of technological change operating

upon a competitive economy. There is no warrant for the assertion
that Marx expected real wages to fall until the entire working class
was at, or below, subsistence level.[77]

In contrast, C. Wright Mills, a friendly critic of Marx, treats the
phrase "growing impoverishment" as a concrete prediction. As if
in refutation of Marx, Mills therefore writes that economic or
material misery "has not increased inside the advanced capitalist
world. On the contrary, the general fact has been an increase in
material standards of living." [78] The position taken here is that
Mills' statement is beside the point because Marx would *not* have
been surprised by this development. Marx simply pointed to a
tendency of the capitalist system in which *constant* capital grew
at a faster rate than *variable* capital. In Marx's view, since the demand for labor is determined not by the total capital but only by
its *variable* component, the demand for the latter increasingly falls
with the increase of the total capital. It falls in direct proportion
to the magnitude of the total capital, and at an accelerated rate,
as this magnitude increases. In other words the size of the labor
force *does* grow with the growth of the total capital but in a constantly diminishing proportion. The working class grows in absolute terms but not relative to the total capital invested in production. Marx wrote: "The laboring population therefore produces, along with the accumulation of capital produced by it, the
means by which itself is made superfluous, is turned into a relative surplus-population; and it does this to an always increasing
extent." [79] This is a statement to be understood in the framework
of Marx's model. The general movement and fluctuation of wages
was to be explained *ideally* by the expansion and contraction of
the industrial reserve army, and Lichtheim is therefore right when
he says that for Marx growing pauperization referred only to the
bottom of the social pyramid. That Marx did not intend this to be
understood as an absolute tendency of the capitalist system may
be seen from the following statement. "The lowest sediment of
the relative surplus-population finally dwells in the sphere of
pauperism . . . . One need only glance superficially at the statistics of English pauperism to find that the quantity of paupers
increases with every crisis, and *diminishes* with every revival of
trade." [80] (Italics mine.) Later in the same section it becomes
even clearer that Marx saw this "law" in a context of "other

things being equal." He wrote: "The more extensive, finally, the lazarus-layers of the working class, and the industrial reserve army, the greater is official pauperism. *This is the absolute general law of capitalist accumulation.* Like all other laws it is modified in its working by many circumstances, the analysis of which does not concern us here." [81] In other words, no sooner has Marx stated the so-called "law" when he immediately adds that it is modified by many circumstances which do not concern him at the moment. This appears to be ample warning not to interpret the law as a concrete prediction.

9. Capitalism is subject to recurrent crises of "overproduction." Such crises, when they become sufficiently disruptive of the system and cause widespread misery, may constitute the necessary but not sufficient condition for the revolution of the proletariat and the change of the system.

Marx's theory of "crisis" is a complicated subject that is rendered even more so by the fact that he never developed it systematically.[82] This has made it extremely difficult even for economists to explicate adequately his approach to the problem. Yet to exclude the subject from the present discussion would be a glaring and unjustifiable omission. That at least a brief consideration of the problem is virtually unavoidable here is made clear by the fact that in the absence of cyclically recurrent and, what is more, worsening crises, Marx had few if any alternative ways of accounting for the "breakdown" of the system.

Scattered and unsystematic as his statements on the subject are, it is still possible to knit them together into a relatively coherent analysis of the phenomenon. Following the logic of Marx's well demonstrated theorem about the historical tendency of the organic composition of capital to rise, it is clear that the demand for labor power must relatively decrease. This demand decreases since it is determined only by the variable component. Ultimately the tendency results in a "surplus" laboring population or an industrial reserve army. In the absence of counteracting factors, e.g., unions, government intervention, etc., this reserve army becomes a lever for depressing wages and contributes to a general depression. In times of prosperity, on the other hand, the reserve army becomes the indispensable source of new labor power.

Marx linked this theorem to another which was generally accepted by economists in his time, namely, the "falling rate of profit." This theorem asserts that it is precisely the competition among capitalists which results in the rising organic composition of capital, or, in other words, which raises the amount of constant capital per man employed. Since it is not constant but variable capital which produces surplus value and profit, there is a tendency for the rate of profit to decline, assuming the rate of surplus-value to remain constant. Marx recognized countervailing tendencies such as the growing productivity of labor-power, but seems to have concluded that this would only retard the decline in the proportion of surplus-value to total capital. Thus he postulated a gradual decline in the rate of profit, leaving open the question of forces operating in the opposite direction, e.g., a higher rate of exploitation which raises the proportion of surplus-value to capital, and increasing productivity which cheapens the elements of constant capital by lowering the value of machinery and raw materials, and in this way changing the organic composition of capital in a direction running opposite to the main tendency.

Under conditions of competition the increasing minimum of capital required with increasing productivity took the following form: As new, more efficient and more expensive capital equipment entered a particular branch of production, it produced the commodities in question at lower costs than the typical or average capitals in that branch. Eventually, however, the newer composition of capital becomes the rule; smaller and less efficient capitals are increasingly crowded out and, assuming a market which does not grow commensurately, there is a crisis of overproduction. This occurs because the total volume of commodities produced is now greater than before, and each capitalist must dispose of a greater volume in order to realize his investment and make a profit. Since the expansion of the market does not keep pace with the expansion of production, commodities accumulate unsold, the market is glutted and production grinds to a halt—if only temporarily. Ultimately this kind of crisis is "caused" by the inability of the producers to consume what they produce or by the "underconsumption" of the masses. As Marx wrote: "It is sheer tautology to say that crises are caused by the scarcity of effective consumption, or of effective consumers. The capitalist system does not know any other modes of consumption than effective ones . . . . That commodities are unsaleable means only that no effective purchasers have been found for them . . . ." [83] Under capitalism there can be no guarantee that effective purchasers will be present when needed. There is no way that the system can guarantee that every sale will be a purchase and every purchase a sale. Marx ridiculed as dogma the view which asserted the contrary and which concluded that circulation of commodities necessarily implies an equilibrium. He wrote: "If the split between the sale and purchase becomes too pronounced, the intimate connection between them, their oneness, asserts itself by producing—a crisis." [84] Basically, then, as Marx saw it the causation involved in such a crisis took the following form: Capitalist accumulation is governed by the search for profit, the satisfaction of wants being only a by-product of this process. Production is therefore divorced from consumption, and though the two are brought together by market mechanisms, the latter operate so haphazardly that they can ensure an equilibrium between supply and demand only at the cost of periodic disruptions in which "superfluous" capital is destroyed and a large number of smaller uncompetitive firms are forced out of production. This kind of crisis may therefore be explained as a result of the disparity between production and consumption, and may be described as a crisis of "underconsumption." However, there is still another approach which Marx took to the problem.

Crises could and did arise from "disproportionality" among the various lines of production themselves. Marx saw the economy divided into two basic departments of production: (a) production of the means of production and (b) production of the means of consumption. Crises of "disproportionality" came about due to the lack of proportion which frequently arose within the first department itself—though, of course, this was never independent of the second department. According to Marx, capitalists cannot possibly know the proper proportions because no master plan exists. This is the condition which he described as "anarchy" of production. The proper proportions have to be discovered by trial and error. To illustrate the phenomenon, if capitalists in the steel industry overestimate the demand for steel and produce more than the market can absorb at profitable prices, they will reduce production and in this way correspondingly reduce the demand for labor-power, coal, iron, etc. Under captialism there is no reason to assume that there will simultaneously take place an expansion in the production of other commodities to compensate for the decline in steel production. The circulation process is consequently disrupted and, depending on the importance of steel, the disruption can precipitate a chain reaction ending in a general crisis. For Marx, "disproportionality is always a possible cause of crisis, and it is almost certainly a complicating factor in all crises whatever their basic cause may be." [85]

The two views—underconsumption and disproportionality—while not necessarily mutually opposed, have political implications which may be so. Indeed, Marxists, after Marx, have been divided precisely on the opposing courses of action suggested in the two views. If the rate of profit is truly falling and if consumption *must* lag more and more behind production, then the system can be expected to become increasingly unstable. Each crisis then becomes a sign that the system is in its death throes and will soon afford the opportunity to burst asunder the capitalist property relations. On the other hand, if, as the second view implies, crises are really caused only by disproportionalities in the production process, then crises do not really threaten the existing social order. All that is necessary is a better understanding of economic processes and the utilization of this knowledge toward the elimination of disproportionality by planning. This does not require a revolution; it can be accomplished under capitalism.

It is the second development which is in fact becoming characteristic of 20th-century capitalism. Industry has become organized into large corporations and trusts, government is increasingly supervising economic processes and indeed "anarchy" of production is increasingly eliminated by that very same government intervention. While this is true it is equally true that it was precisely in the 20th century that capitalism was hit by the most severe and most widespread crisis in its history. One can therefore readily understand those Marxists who, with the "crash" of 1929 and the depression that followed, tended to accept the first view and prepared for a revolutionary change of the system. This did not take place and instead the advanced capitalist countries weathered the crisis by means of systematic government intervention and war. The United States, for example, pulled out of the depression only during World War II.

Whether or not the stabilization of advanced capitalism can be ensured is even now impossible to ascertain. Probably few if any economists would altogether rule out the possibility of severe economic crises in the future. Matters are complicated today by developments which Marx never foresaw: The rise of the Soviet bloc of nations whose existence is relevant to the economic future of capitalism; the increasing rationalization of the capitalist economy by corporations, trade associations and state intervention; the role of artificially stimulated demands, e.g., status obsolescence and mass advertising in stabilizing the economy; and, finally, the preparation for war. Under these circumstances there is presently almost no way of knowing if and when crises will occur and what consequences they may bring. In the light of present developments, however, it would indeed appear that Marx underestimated the capacity of capitalism to recover from crises and overestimated their revolutionizing effect on the working class. For until now in the history of capitalism, crises have not resulted anywhere in the revolutionary change of the system.

10. As a consequence of their exploitation at the hands of the owners, the workers, a "class-in-itself," will become a "class-for-itself."

For Marx, the phrase "class-in-itself" refers to the objective aspect of class, i.e., an aggregate of workers having a common relationship to the means of production. This is what Max Weber later described as an aggregate of persons or families occupying a similar position in the economic structure, their life chances therefore being determined by their economic position. The phrase "class-for-itself" refers to the situation in which the workers develop solidarity or class consciousness, i.e., an awareness of their objective position and interests. For Marx this did not refer to association for merely economic ends. The criterion of class-consciousness was the organization of political parties representative of working-class interests by which the workers could achieve power. Therefore, insofar as throughout capitalist countries labor and working-class parties have come into being[86]—assuming they are in some degree representative of working-class interests—

Marx's prediction has come true. Intermittently in the history of European countries such labor parties have been voted into power and have attempted to reshape their respective economies. Workers have organized politically and have taken power, but not through revolutionary insurgency.

However, a more complex problem is hidden in the phrase "class-for-itself." If it is taken to mean long-run, general, and rational interests, then who is to be the judge of them, the workers themselves or an outside leadership group? C. Wright Mills has pointed up the moral implications of Marx's occasional ambiguity on this score. Marx did not adequately "consider the difference between (a) What is to the Interests of Men according to an analysis of their position in society, and (b) What Men are Interested In according to the men themselves." [87] Despite this ambiguity, there is good reason to believe that he would have abhorred an *élitist* approach to the workers in which one would impose upon them what one thought was best for them.

Marx held the conviction throughout his life that the workers would have to emancipate themselves. As we have seen, not only in his later writings on the Commune, where he insisted on the democratic character of the Dictatorship of the Proletariat, but in the *Manifesto* as well, Marx plainly stated:

> [Communists] have no interests apart from those of the working class as a whole.
> They do not put forward any sectarian principles in accordance with which they wish to mold the proletarian movement.[88]

Of course, this still leaves open the problem of what the rational interests of the workers are. It is at least in part a moral judgment to determine what is "rational," and whether class interests are to be the only, or even the major, rational interests. Marx seems to have overlooked this.

From his standpoint, capitalism was systematically deforming and debasing the workers, mentally as well as physically. Most of their waking hours were spent in misery and there seemed to be no escaping this fate without transforming the entire social order. Surely, the workers would recognize this with time. Man is both rational and perfectible, and he will not tolerate for long a situation which violates his nature. Marx's faith in these premises of the Enlightenment was perhaps too strong; for although he acknowledged that men were occasionally possessed by "false consciousness"—a blindness to their true class interests—he regarded this as a temporary condition which would inevitably yield to "true consciousness" based upon reason and experience. In these terms, it would be true to say that Marx's mood obscured from his view the fact that workers often favored other interests over class interests.

11. The greater the functional indispensability of a class in the economic system, the greater its political power in the society as a whole.

This proposition, though nowhere explicitly stated by Marx, is a justifiable inference from the historical role which he assigned to the proletariat under capitalism. However, he seems to have arrived at this conclusion from the history of the bourgeoisie. Marx saw each step in the economic development of the capitalist class accompanied by a corresponding political advance. An oppressed class under the domination of the feudal lords, it fought its way upward until, with the rise of large-scale industry and the establishment of the world market, it achieved hegemony in the modern representative state. Similarly, Marx believed, with the advance of capitalism, the potential economic power and indispensability of the workers will lead to their political ascendancy; while the bourgeoisie's increasingly "parasitic" role will lead to its political decline.

To what extent Marx's conclusions about the role of the proletariat were based on independent empirical analysis of the workings of the capitalist system, and to what extent on historical analogy is difficult to determine. The analogy, however, is an untenable one. For as M. M. Bober has convincingly argued: "The ancient slave did not erect the feudal system, nor the serf or journeyman the capitalist system. History does not demonstrate that the exploited class of one society is the architect of the next social organization." [89] The struggle between the serfs and nobles did not bring about capitalism. And with respect to the bourgeoisie, it was *in* feudal society but in a sense not *of* it. The bourgeois system grew up as a relatively independent structure within feudalism. When the bourgeoisie became sufficiently powerful economically and politically, it did away with the various privileges of the nobles and established a system in accordance with its own interests. In contrast, the workers and capitalists are part of the same economic system, and the former are not representative of any independent economic system. In addition, whereas the bourgeoisie was an economically and politically expanding class before the French Revolution, for example, the workers in 20th-century capitalism have declined in both respects.

12. In capitalist society, as in class societies generally, the state represents the interests of the propertied classes and serves as their coercive instrument.

Marx was on rather firm ground when he made this allegation about the state apparatus of 19th-century European societies. In the present century too, in the United States as well as in Europe —not to speak of the other areas of the world—industrial history provided ample evidence to support the assertion that the state exercises a protective and coercive function in behalf of the advantaged and propertied classes. That this has been *one* function of the state in the history of capitalism is relatively clear. That it has been the *only* function is very doubtful indeed. Today in the advanced industrial societies it is evident that the state bureaucracy does more than merely manage the affairs, and ensure the domination, of the corporate and other rich. Equally important is the fact that various other groups and organized publics have managed to gain in influence upon the state. Moreover, in societies without so-called propertied classes the state does not "wither away."

In studying the role of the state, it would seem that "power elite" is a more useful concept than "ruling class." That the wealthy class is also the ruling one should not be a dogmatic assumption but a hypothesis. Lumping together economic and political elements in one concept, as in "ruling class" ("ruling" referring to power, and "class" to ownership of property), renders the formulation of a hypothesis much more difficult. On the other hand, the concept "power elite" leaves empirically open the question of the economic determination of power and the problem of the relative weight of the wealthy classes within the higher political circles. The element of truth in Marx's proposition is that the control of productive resources and other property provides for control of men as well as things. This must be immediately qualified, however, by pointing to the various forces, notably trade-unions and other veto-groups, which countervail against the power of property as represented by the state.

By treating power as economically determined, the relatively more autonomous role, especially in the 20th century, of the two very powerful institutional orders, namely, the political and the military, is neglected. If the state is defined as an instrument of the economically powerful class, it obscures the variety of relations between economic classes and the power they hold, thus solving by definition a problem which is an empirical one. On the other hand, if, following Weber, the state is defined as an organization which monopolizes "the use of legitimate force over a given territory," [90] then the relationship of propertied classes to any given state can become an empirical problem.

13. The working class will seize power, either peacefully or by force, and establish a dictatorship of the proletariat, a democratic transition phase between capitalism and communism.

Clearly this has not occurred in any of the advanced capitalist countries in which Marx anticipated it. Those societies in which revolutions have occurred, and in which so-called proletarian dictatorships have been established, are quite different from the ones Marx had in mind. Consideration of these societies, the course they have followed, and their relationship to Marx's theory, would constitute a full-scale study in itself and therefore will not occupy us here.

To summarize, if Marx's theories have not been wholly verified by historical developments since his time, they contain many fruitful leads. The nature of Marx's hypotheses, pertaining to whole societies as they do, makes it exceedingly difficult to "test" them. The necessary techniques were not available in his time nor are they available in ours. Nevertheless, the selected major propositions discussed above may constitute an important source for more precise, smaller, and, consequently, more easily verifiable propositions.

At the center of Marx's thought stands the working class, the dynamic actor of the capitalist system and its main agency of change. If until now this agency has failed to meet Marx's expectations, what is the probability of its doing so in the future? To answer this question, Marx's conception of the system and the role of the working class within it, must once more be examined.

REFLECTIONS ON MARX'S AGENCY OF CHANGE

It will be recalled that Marx saw at least three phases in the development of the capitalist mode of production: simple cooperation, manufacture, and machinery in modern industry. The central characteristic of this mode of production was the constant growth of the productive forces within it. Marx emphasized this characteristic with the proposition that the "bourgeoisie cannot exist without constantly revolutionizing the instruments of production, and thereby the relations of production, and with them the whole relations of society." [91] Along with this proposition Marx put forward a second important one, namely, that the capitalist mode of production was eliminating all older and intermediate classes and strata and that the "proletariat alone is really revolutionary. The other classes decay and finally disappear in the face of modern industry; the proletariat is its special and essential product." [92]

It is quite clear that Marx expected the changes within the system to lead to a change *of* the system while the proletariat was still a large and growing force within capitalist society. At the same time Marx saw a countervailing tendency, i.e., production workers themselves being increasingly displaced by machines, thus leading to the formation of an industrial reserve army. Marx lived in a period of capitalism's rapid expansion and therefore saw, as was previously indicated, an absolute growth in the size of the working class in spite of its diminishing role in production relative to machines. He anticipated a change *of* the system long before this class would begin to dwindle, and it is for this reason that the working-class, as the chief agency of change, remained at the center of his revolutionary theory. Marx understood only *some* of the implications of the perfecting of machinery in industry and the extent to which this process was making human labor superfluous. He never foresaw the dimensions of this process as it is taking place today, nor did he believe that such changes could take place while the capitalist system persisted. This process is taking a special form today and is termed *automation*. The emergence of automation, its impact on the existing social organization, and some of its implications for Marx's theory, will be our main concern in the present discussion.

The central proposition put forward and explored here is that automation constitutes a qualitative departure from the more conventional advance of technology and that it constitutes a *fourth and critical phase* in the growth of productive forces under capitalism. Marx did not foresee this phase and did not, of course, build it into his model. This suggests one of two possibilities: (a) Either Marx's model together with his theories about the role of the working class are superseded by present trends in the capitalist system and are therefore obsolete, or (b) the present trend—albeit in a form different from which he imagined—will lead to some of the "revolutionary" consequences during the fourth phase in the development of the capitalist mode of production which Marx expected in the third. In a word, not the third but the fourth phase may be the critical one.

With the introduction and development of production by machines, work was made available to a huge pool of unskilled persons who in the main had migrated from rural areas to the cities. Today, it is precisely these unskilled, together with semi-skilled and even management personnel, who are poured back into the pool. The application of machinery in large-scale industry, e.g., mass-production in assembly lines, etc., absorbed increasingly large masses of *unskilled* workers. Automation, on the other hand, cannot absorb them under any circumstances.

What makes automation different from the previous phases in capitalist production? Until recently, industry, whether based on cooperation, division of labor, or modern machine production, was man-centered. Men were at the center of the production process; they were essential both to operation and control, and more or less the makers of their products. It is for this reason that Marx regarded the increasing application of machinery to production as the increasing productivity of labor. With automation, however, "man not only loses irrevocably his function as *homo faber;* he no longer even possesses the character of *animal laborans.*" [93] Instead, as Ben Seligman and others have observed, he is a sometime supervisor of a process over which he has no control. Actual control is carried out by electronic systems whose feedbacks **and** servomechanisms make it possible to produce goods and manipulate information in a continuous system without human participation.

There appear to be four basic principles which underlie automation. Two of these have been basic to industrial production for some time; the other two were introduced only recently. A definition of automation rests on all four and, in fact, the four taken together are what make it a new phenomenon. The principles are: (a) mechanization, (b) rationalization, (c) feedback, and (d) continuous process.[94] Mechanization refers simply to the substitution of machinery for human or animal labor and muscle, as with the steam engine, for example. Rationalization refers to the application of reason to the solution of problems or to the search for knowledge. Mechanization and rationalization have been used in various combinations in conventional productive processes until recently. The third and fourth principles, when combined in a new synthesis with the first two, impart a unique character to the technology of automation. These are *feedback* and *continuous flow*. Feedback is a concept of control whereby the input of machines is regulated by the machine's own output so that the output meets the conditions of a predetermined objective. Finally, there is the principle of continuous flow; production becomes an endless process. When automation is successfully applied to production, the following seem to be the direct effects:

(a) Many direct production jobs are abolished.

(b) A smaller number of newer jobs are created, requiring different, and mostly higher skills, e.g., equipment maintenance and design, systems analysis, programming and engineering.

(c) The requirements of some of the remaining jobs are raised. For example, the integration of several formerly separate processes and the enhanced value of capital investment increase the need for comprehension and far-sightedness on the part of management.

What is the effect of the new technology on "production workers" as Marx understood the term? They are being eliminated at an unprecedented rate. A million and a half jobs disappeared between 1953 and 1960.[95] There are no new sectors, as yet, which can absorb these "superfluous" workers and few prospects of such sectors opening in the future with the possible exception of state-sponsored welfare projects. In addition, it appears that under the new circumstances unions will become increasingly more helpless since their production-base is declining and they are, as a consequence, growing progressively weaker as a political force within the society.

Besides the worker who is immediately affected, it seems that the "new middle class" is also affected by automation. The function of the middle-manager, for example, is increasingly usurped by the computer, and this usurpation has far-reaching consequences for the entire executive structure. With the elimination of the middle echelons the men at the top increase their power and achieve greater control over the decision-making process. The corporate structure becomes more formal. The number of links in the chain of command is reduced drastically. According to Herbert A. Simon of the Carnegie Institute of Technology, by 1985 machines will be able to dispense with all middle echelons in business.[96] Production planning will be increasingly given over to the computer while the middle-manager will join the worker in the ranks of the unemployed.

Automation accelerates the concentration of production in the hands of fewer and fewer large corporations. Carl Dreher has observed that those corporations "will automate who have the resources and the hardihood, and from those who have not will be taken away even that which they have. It will be an automation shakeout, and it will hit the smallest hardest." [97] Thus it can be expected, as automation proceeds, that production will become more and more concentrated in the larger firms. While the scale of production grows, and with it the size of establishments and the capital employed in them, the number of workers will decline. Shifting workers to clerical, service, and other jobs will not be possible since these areas are increasingly automated themselves.

Simultaneously with the decline in the number of production workers, and thus of union membership, the unions will find fewer but more powerful corporate antagonists. The production-base of the unions will become narrower, weaker, and thus less effective. What does this imply with respect to the conventional weapons of unions, the strike, for example? There is every reason to believe that it will lose its effectiveness in an era when a handful of supervisory employees are able to keep up full-scale production. It is therefore highly probable that the structure of the working class and the unions will change radically.

With the development of automation the polarization of the social structure may now take place which Marx predicted would take place earlier. How far will these changes go? There is reason to believe that they will go quite far. The new technology will create millions of unskilled "misfits," people who would not be employable in advanced industries and would therefore have no way of sharing in the benefits of increased productivity. The bulk of these people will become and remain either totally unemployed or a low-wage labor force for a sector of marginal, substandard industries. On the other side there would tend to emerge a professional, educated, and skilled elite garnering most of the benefits of increased productivity and shaping its own distinctive style of life. A dichotomy of this sort, once established, might perpetuate itself and create a new form of caste society.[98]

A caste society is one possible consequence of the widening chasm between the educated elite and the unskilled. On the other hand, the polarization of the social structure was one basis for the revolutionary changes of capitalist society which Marx expected. This process of polarization could conceivably have the revolutionary consequences in the fourth phase which Marx predicted for the third. The social base of this "revolution" would consist of the unemployed, the ill-educated, and the entire residue of human beings not needed by the corporate machine. As one social scientist has observed, this "revolution—with or without violence, whether from the left or from the right—will only be averted if the corporation can make room in its environs for those who demand entry." [99]

The facts clearly suggest that, at least in the advanced industrial societies, the working class may have lost its "historic opportunity" for revolution if indeed it ever had it. As the new technology gathers momentum, the working class will increasingly lose its significance. This class, and the place it occupies in Marx's theory of revolution, is quite different from that new "residue" of ill-educated and unemployed—a new *lumpenproletariat*—which may result from the new productive forces in this fourth critical phase.

Of course, there is no need to draw pessimistic conclusions about the social consequences of the new technology, no need to assume that matters must go that far. Some observers have suggested that the new technology constitutes a scientific-industrial revolution which can provide the technical basis—the necessary but not sufficient condition—of a new civilization.

These observers have subjected present institutional arrangements to a fundamental re-examination in the light of the rapidly growing new technology, and they have concluded that the present arrangements along with the prevailing value system are basically incompatible with the requirements of the technological revolution taking place before our very eyes. Consciously or not, they have applied to present conditions Marx's theory of social change in which the tension between the growing "productive forces" and the existing "relations of production" accounts for the nature and direction of basic changes in whole societies. In these terms, the new productive forces—automation and cybernation—are viewed as rendering the present institutional structure obsolete and therefore requiring basic alterations. Major desirable social changes are now becoming possible, it is argued, and therefore ought to be introduced and instituted. With time, the entire social order could be transformed and become a "world more attractive." The suggested changes pertain to *work, education,* and *leisure,* and do not necessarily depend on the older socialistic notions of abolishing private property as an institution and replacing it with public ownership.

The "new" ideas about these three spheres—work, education, and leisure—are indeed "utopian," but not in any quixotic or romantic sense of the term. They are utopian in Karl Mannheim's sense:

> Only those orientations transcending reality will be referred to by us as utopian which, when they pass over into conduct, tend to shatter, either partially or wholly, the order of things prevailing at the time.[100]

Work, it is argued, need no longer be alienated labor. The notion, still prevalent, that man was created for labor, and not the reverse, is now an antiquated one. Alienated labor, a primary condition of our general malaise, considerably reinforced by that religious ethic which dictates that man pursue intrinsically ungratifying tasks in a morally dutiful manner, is now a form of self-imposed and unnecessary servitude. The emancipation of men from this condition, the utopian orientations suggest, is now a real possibility. An example of one such orientation is the idea advanced by the economist, Robert Theobald.

> We are trapped in a socio-economic system which only works if it provides jobs for everyone. One of the speakers believes that the recent measure put forward by Senator Clark and others to insure full employment represents an advance. I consider it a retrograde step. I want to move toward full *un*employment. I want a society in which nobody will toil, in which people will not have to do things they do not want to do simply in order to make money. It is my belief that the cybernated machine system provides the potential for adequate incomes for all if we are willing to utilize it properly. I believe that this must be our aim because we cannot keep the existing system operating too much longer . . . .
>
> A society which insists that everyone should earn his living at a time when this is not necessary is perpetuating a type of slavery.[101]

Such orientations have innumerable implications, not only for changes in the world of work, but also for the transformation of the character of man. The educational system would be redesigned to prepare for the fulfillment not of tasks, functions, and occupations, in the accepted sense, but rather to create a new man who, in addition to acquiring expert knowledge in any sphere he should choose, would become genuinely capable of using the leisure time now at hand, and hence free to realize himself as a human being.

A contemporary philosopher, Herbert Marcuse, has grasped the connection between the new technology and freedom.

> Automation, once it becomes *the* process of material production, would revolutionize the whole society. The reification of human labor power, driven to perfection, would shatter the reified form by cutting the chain that ties the individual to the machinery—the mechanism through which his own labor enslaves him. Complete automation in the realm of necessity would open the dimension of free time as the one in which man's private *and* societal existence would constitute itself. This would be the historical transcendence toward a new civilization.[102]

Marx's conception of the capitalist system has been critically examined and its deficiencies have been indicated. He misjudged the political effects of the main trends in the economic foundation of capitalism; he entertained a rationalist bias in his political and psychological theory; his conception of power and the state is one-sided. In spite of its future-piercing aspects, Marx's thinking reflects 19th-century capitalism and for that reason is now inadequate.

Does this mean, however, that his social and political theories are now totally obsolete and worthless? The answer as I hope to show is decidedly in the negative. Marx's theoretical framework remains one of the most fruitful for thinking about man, society and history. In what follows, his general theory is again reviewed but this time with the emphasis on its heuristic value. Then Marx's best-known "journalistic" writings are examined for the light they throw on his own attempts to apply his so-called materialist conception to the revolutionary political events of his time. These writings reveal, among other things, that in Marx's application of his general principles to specific problems, political events are not treated as mere epiphenomena—as simple effects of economic causes. And this is something one could hardly learn from his general theory alone.

NOTES

1. Karl Marx, *Wage Labor and Capital* in Marx and Engels, *Selected Works*, Vol. I. Moscow: Foreign Languages Publishing House, 1950, p. 83. Writings from the *Selected Works* are hereafter cited as MESW.

2. Karl Marx, *The Poverty of Philosophy*. Moscow: Foreign Languages Publishing House, N.D., p. 127.

3. Marx, *Wage Labour and Capital,* MESW I, pp. 83-84.

4. *Ibid.,* p. 84.

5. Karl Marx, *A Contribution to the Critique of Political Economy*. Chicago: Charles H. Kerr and Company, 1904, pp. 11-12. Here a note is necessary, I believe, about the way certain key predicates in these propositions have traditionally been translated from the original German. The sentence above which reads: "The mode of production in material life *determines* the general character of the social, political and spiritual processes, etc.," appears in the German thus: "Die Produktionsweise des materiellen Lebens *bedingt* den sozialen, politischen und geistigen Lebensprozess uberhaupt." Here *bedingt* is translated as "determines." The very next sentence reads in English thus: "It is not the consciousness of men that determines their existence, but, on the contrary, their social existence determines

their consciousness." This appears in the German as: "Es ist nicht das Bewusstsein der Menschen, das ihr Sein, sondern umgekert ihr gesellschaftliches Sein, das ihr Bewusstsein *bestimmt*." Here we will note that both *bedingt* and *bestimmt* are rendered by the English "determines." Although Cassell's German Dictionary translates *bestimmt* as "determines," it does not offer this translation for *bedingt* which is translated as "limit, restrict; cause, occasion." It would seem, however, that for our purposes "determines" is a satisfactory translation since it imputes to "mode of production" and to "social existence" the "causal priority" that Marx intended in this formulation. For the original German text, see Karl Marx, Friedrich Engels, *Werke,* Band 13. Berlin: Dietz Verlag, 1961, pp. 8-9.

6. Karl Marx and Frederick Engels, *The German Ideology.* New York: International Publishers, 1960, p. 18.

7. *Ibid.,* p. 202.

8. For example, see Engels' letter to J. Bloch of September 21-22, 1890, and his letter to H. Starkenburg of January 25, 1899 in MESW II, pp. 443 and 457, respectively. To Bloch, Engels wrote: "The economic situation is the basis, but the various elements of the superstructure . . . also exercise their influence upon the course of the historical struggles and in many cases preponderate in determining their form." In his letter to Starkenburg he wrote: "Political, juridical, philosophical, religious, literary, artistic, etc., development is based on economic development. But all these react upon one another and also upon the economic basis. It is not that the economic condition is the *cause* and *alone active,* while everything else only has a passive effect. There is, rather, interaction on the basis of economic necessity, which ultimately always asserts itself."

9. Marx, *Capital* Vol. I. Moscow: Foreign Language Publishing House, 1954, pp. 714-715.

10. *Ibid.,* pp. 715-716.

11. Ryazanoff edition (New York: International Publishers Co., Inc., 1930), pp. 25-54. An additional reason for the use of the *Manifesto* is that it contains Marx's theoretical conclusions prior to the various European revolutions of 1848, the coup d'état of Louis Napoleon, and, finally, the *Paris Commune* of 1871.

12. Frederick Engels, *The Origin of the Family, Private Property and the State.* New York: International Publishers, 1942, p. 155.

13. *Ibid.,* p. 82.

14. *Ibid.,* p. 145.

15. *Ibid.,* p. 155.

16. *Ibid.,* p. 156.

17. *Ibid.,* p. 158.

18. MESW I, p. 21.

19. Marx, *The Civil War in France,* MESW I, p. 468.

20. Marx's letter to Kugelman, MESW II, p. 420.

21. For an illuminating discussion of this point see Sherman H. M. Chang, *The Marxian Theory of the State*. Philadelphia: John Spencer, Inc., 1931, pp. 74-75.

22. Marx's letter to Weydemeyer, MESW II, p. 410.

23. Marx, *Critique of the Gotha Program*, MESW II, p. 30.

24. MESW I, p. 440.

25. Marx, *Manifesto*, p. 141.

26. C. Wright Mills, *The Marxists*. New York: Dell Publishing Co., 1962, p. 106.

27: Karl Marx and Frederick Engels, *Selected Correspondence*. Moscow: Foreign Languages Publishing House, 1953, p. 540.

28. *Ibid.*, p. 379.

29. *Ibid.*, p. 412.

30. See Ephraim Fischoff, "The History of a Controversy," in *Protestantism and Capitalism: The Weber Thesis and Its Critics*. Edited by Robert W. Green. Boston: D. C. Heath and Company, 1959, pp. 107-114.

31. R. H. Tawney in his Foreword to Max Weber, *The Protestant Ethic and the Spirit of Capitalism*. Translated by Talcott Parsons. New York: Charles Scribner's Sons, 1958, p. 1 (c).

32. See Max Weber, *General Economic History*. Translated by Frank H. Knight. New York: Collier Books, 1961, from which the following discussion is summarized.

33. *Ibid.*, p. 259.

34. *Ibid.*, p. 260.

35. *Ibid.*, p. 260.

36. *Ibid.*, p. 260.

37. See Fischoff, *op. cit.*, p. 110.

38. *Ibid.*, p. 111.

39. See Tawney's Foreword to *The Protestant Ethic*, p. 8.

40. *Ibid.*, p. 8.

41. *Ibid.*, p. 9.

42. *Ibid.*, p. 9.

43. R. H. Tawney, *Religion and the Rise of Capitalism*. New York: Mentor Books, 1953, pp. 76-77.

44. Wilbert E. Moore, *Industrialization and Labor: Social Aspects of Economic Development*. Ithaca and New York: Cornell University Press, 1951, p. 5.

45. *Ibid.*, p. 7.

46. This point is further elaborated in a later discussion.

47. C. W. Mills, *White Collar*. New York: Oxford University Press, 1956, p. 13.

48. *Final Report of the Select Committee on Small Business*, to the House of Representatives, 87th Congress, House Report No. 2569, January 3, 1963, pp. 22-23.

49. Mills, *The Marxists*, p. 107.

50. *Ibid.,* p. 107.

51. Ralf Dahrendorf, *Class and Class Conflict in Industrial Society.* Stanford, California: Stanford University Press, 1959, p. 258.

52. Marx in a letter to Weydemeyer, MESW II, p. 410.

53. Joseph A. Schumpeter, *Capitalism, Socialism and Democracy.* New York and Evanston: Harper & Row Publishers, 1962, p. 19.

54. See, for example, the discussion of the relationship of the two classes in F. W. Taylor, "The Principles of Scientific Management," *Scientific Management.* New York and London, 1947, p. 10.

55. Schumpeter, *op. cit.,* pp. 19-20.

56. Marx, MESW I, p. 134.

57. *Ibid.,* p. 147.

58. Frederich Engels, *Germany: Revolution and Counter-Revolution* in *Karl Marx, Selected Works,* Vol. II. New York: International Publishers, N.D., p. 127.

59. Marx, *Capital* I, p. 481.

60. *Ibid.,* p. 494.

61. Engels, MESW I, p. 118.

62. *Ibid.,* p. 118.

63. See Selig Perlman, *A Theory of the Labor Movement.* New York: Augustus M. Kelley, 1949, pp. 230-250.

64. Seymour Martin Lipset, *Political Man.* Garden City, New York: Anchor Books, 1963, p. 230.

65. *Ibid.,* p. 234.

66. *Ibid.,* p. 230. In citing Lipset's view I am merely trying to illustrate the fact that some contemporary social scientists find it useful to interpret even American politics on the basis of class and class interest.

67. Robert M. MacIver, *The Web of Government.* New York: Macmillan, 1947, p. 315.

68. See Talcott Parsons, "Voting and the Equilibrium of the American Political System," in E. Burdick and A. Brodbeck (eds.), *American Voting Behavior.* Glencoe: The Free Press, 1959, p. 88.

69. *Ibid.,* pp. 88-89.

70. Mills, *The Marxists,* p. 108.

71. Karl Marx, *Critique of the Gotha Program,* MESW II, p. 20.

72. One of the most comprehensive discussions of these trends is presented in C. Wright Mills, *White Collar,* passim.

73. Joseph A. Schumpeter, *Capitalism, Socialism and Democracy.* New York: Harper & Row, Publishers, 1962, p. 34.

74. Paul M. Sweezy, *The Theory of Capitalist Development.* New York: Monthly Review Press, 1956, p. 18.

75. *Ibid.,* p. 19.

76. George Lichtheim, *Marxism, An Historical and Critical Study.* New York: Frederick A. Praeger, 1962, p. 189.

77. *Ibid.,* p. 189.

78. Mills, *The Marxists,* p. 11.

79. *Marx, Capital* I, p. 631.

80. *Ibid.,* p. 643.

81. *Ibid.,* p. 644.

82. There is agreement among Marx's critics that the question of crisis cannot be understood adequately from Marx's writings alone. Sweezy, for example, has argued that there can be "no question of treating crises within the general framework of Marxian economics without taking account of the writings of later Marxists on the subject." For a scholarly account of the contributions of Eduard Bernstein, Tugan-Baranowsky, Conrad Schmidt, Karl Kautsky, Louis B. Boudin, Rosa Luxembourg, Henryk Grossman, et. al., see Sweezy, *op. cit.,* Chapter XI, The Breakdown Controversy, pp. 190-213.

83. Marx, *Capital* Vol. II. Moscow: Foreign Languages Publishing House, 1960, p. 410.

84. *Capital* I, p. 114.

85. Sweezy, *op. cit.,* p. 157.

86. The United States is a conspicuous exception here. As was pointed out in the discussion of Lipset's thesis, however, one can discern in the United States the functional equivalent of a labor party in certain sections of the Democratic Party which the lower classes have tended historically to support.

87. Mills, *The Marxists,* p. 114.

88. Marx, *Communist Manifesto,* MESW I, p. 44.

89. M. M. Bober, *Karl Marx's Interpretation of History,* 2nd ed., Rev. Cambridge, Mass.: Harvard Economic Studies, Vol. 31, 1948, p. 340.

90. H. H. Gerth and C. Wright Mills, *From Max Weber: Essays in Sociology.* New York: Oxford University Press, 1958, p. 48.

91. Marx, *Manifesto,* MESW I, p. 36.

92. *Ibid.,* p. 42.

93. Ben Seligman, "Man Work and the Automated Feast," *Commentary,* July, 1962, p. 10.

94. See Walter S. Buckingham's, discussion in *Hearings Before the Sub-Committee on Economic Stabilization,* 84th Congress, Washington, D. C., October, 1955, pp. 31-32.

95. Seligman, *op. cit.,* p. 14.

96. *Ibid.,* p. 14.

97. Carl Dreher, *Automation.* New York: Norton, 1957, p. 115.

98. See the discussion of this possibility in the United States, in Model, Roland, and Stone, *The Scientific-Industrial Revolution.* New York: 1957, p. 45.

99. Andrew Hacker, "Towards a Corporate America," submitted to the 59th annual conference of the American Political Science Association. Quoted in the *New York Times,* Saturday, September 7, 1963.

100. Karl Mannheim, *Ideology and Utopia.* London: Routledge & Kegan Paul Ltd., 1960, p. 173.

101. Robert Theobald, "Symposium: Johnson's War on Poverty," in *New Politics,* Vol. III, No. 4, Fall 1964, pp. 14-15.

102. Herbert Marcuse, *One Dimensional Man.* Boston: Beacon Press, 1964, pp. 36-37.

IV. Theory as a Guide to the Study of Society

THE HEURISTIC VALUE OF THE THEORY

IN THE DISCUSSION OF MARX'S THEORY IN THE PREVIOUS CHAPTER, his propositions were treated as he stated them, i.e., unequivocally assigning the determining influence to the productive forces and the economic foundation. There it was pointed out that Marx intended his theory as a historically specific proposition applicable primarily to England and western Europe. He himself explicitly stated these qualifications: "Hence the 'historical inevitability' of this movement is *expressly* limited to the countries of Western Europe." [1] On the basis of the evidence of these societies, Marx was suggesting that in the *long run* the tension between the productive forces and the property relations had resolved itself in the further development of the productive forces. Although it was advanced on the basis of west-European history, this proposition could serve as a useful hypothesis in guiding investigations elsewhere. In emphasizing the heuristic value of Marx's theory, a slightly modified approach will be taken and here Engels' letters may be more valuable than before. [2]

For Engels the various institutional orders of a society stood in a hierarchic relationship to one another in terms of their mutual influence. Causal priority was assigned to the sphere of production in particular and to the economic order in general; secondary causal influence was assigned to the *political* and *legal* orders; and tertiary influence was imputed to such realms of ideology as the philosophical and religious, etc. Thus in his discussion of the interaction of economic development and state power, for example, Engels saw three possibilities: (1) State power could accelerate economic development; (2) it could retard and oppose such development; and, finally, (3) it could modify the direction and character of this development, the third case eventually reducing itself to one of the former. According to Engels, the interaction took place between two unequal forces—the economic development being stronger in the *long run*. He did not deny, however, "that in cases two and three political power can do great damage to the economic development and cause a great squandering of energy and material." [3]

A similar process takes place in the case of *law*. "As soon as the new division of labor which creates professional lawyers becomes necessary, another new and independent sphere is opened up which, for all its general dependence on production and trade, has also a special capacity for reacting upon these spheres." [4] Clarifying this view further, Engels suggests that ". . . the jurist imagines he is operating with *a priori* propositions, whereas they are really only economic reflexes; so everything is upside down." [5] Moreover, this *"ideological outlook* reacts in turn upon the economic development and may, within certain limits, modify it." [6] In Engels' view, then, the economic structure exercises causal priority "ultimately," or in the long run; the political and legal spheres act back upon the economic structure and in the shorter run modify the course of its development. There is still another realm, i.e., the spheres even more remote from production; these exercise a kind of tertiary influence.

> As to the realms of ideology which soar still higher in the air—religion, philosophy, etc.—these have a prehistoric stock, found already in existence by and taken over in the historical period, of what we should today call bunk. These various false conceptions of nature, of man's own being, of spirits, magic forces, etc., have for the most part only a negative economic element as their basis; the low economic development of the prehistoric period is supplemented and also partially conditioned and even caused by the false conceptions of nature. And even though economic necessity was the main driving force of the progressive knowledge of nature and has become ever more so, it would surely be pedantic to try and find economic causes for all this primitive nonsense. The history of science is the history of the gradual clearing away of this nonsense or rather of its replacement by fresh but always less absurd nonsense. The people who attend to this belong in their turn to special spheres in the division of labor and appear to themselves to

be working in an independent field. And to the extent that they form an independent group within the social division of labor, their productions, including their errors, react upon the whole development of society, even on its economic development. But all the same they themselves are in turn under the dominating influence of economic development.[7]

In these formulations, then, Engels is saying, in effect, that the economic development will assert itself "ultimately," i.e., in the long run. There is no guarantee, however, in any given period— i.e., anything shorter than the so-called *long run*—that the relationship among the various realms will manifest the hierarchic pattern attributed to them as a long-run tendency. This formulation therefore provides little or no guidance in short-run problems and suggests that the most fruitful employment of Marx's theoretical approach is achieved by temporarily leaving open the relation among the separate spheres, i.e., making an empirical problem of their mutual relationship. This approach enjoins the student to focus attention on the economic sphere while examining its relation to the others. This is the heuristic value of Marx's materialist conception. In his analyses of the events of his time, as in the case of his journalistic writings, Marx employs his conception in this fashion; he does not automatically assume that political events are always effects of economic causes. On the contrary, he treats such relationships empirically and even traces the influence of political on economic events—a fact not at all deducible from his general theoretical formulations. Therefore, by comparing the theoretical with the journalistic writings, it will become clear that his conception of society, and the historical change it underwent, was to be regarded above all as a "guide to study, not a lever for construction after the Hegelian." [8]

The Theoretical Writings

In his preface to *A Contribution to the Critique of Political Economy,* Marx wrote that "legal relations as well as forms of state could neither be understood by themselves, nor explained by the so-called general progress of the human mind. . . ." [9] This, in its time, was a proposition of revolutionary significance for social science.[10] To grasp that the various institutional orders of society are interdependent and do not enjoy a completely autonomous development was a seminal discovery. He developed this theory in a number of explicit propositions and these in turn guided his studies throughout his life. What are these propositions? To answer this question we must cover some of the same ground as before.

1. In social production men enter into certain definite relations that are indispensable and independent of their will.

2. These relations in turn correspond to a definite phase in the growth of the socially productive forces.

3. The totality of these relations of production is in fact the social basis of various forms of social consciousness generally, and of legal and political superstructures in particular.

4. The rate of development of the productive forces gives some indication of the compatibility of the prevailing relations of production or property relations.

5. At a given point, the productive forces come in conflict with the existing property relations. The latter are no longer compatible with the growing productive forces and no longer provide a framework for their uninterrupted growth.

6. This conflict results in a crisis and in a period of social revolution. Social revolution means that all aspects of the society are eventually changed; the economic foundation, the character of social relations, and the cultural content of the society are transformed.

These six theoretical statements are Marx's working hypotheses which may apply to societies in general. They may be employed in the study of the structure, and processes of change, of any society. How may the major social changes, whose mechanics are described in the fifth and sixth hypotheses, be studied? Marx answers this question also in general terms.

1. In considering social change, a distinction must always be made between the "material transformation of the economic conditions of production which can be determined with the precision of natural science, and the legal, political, religious, aesthetic or philosophic—in short, ideological forms in which men become conscious of this conflict and fight it out." [11]

2. Do not judge a society in a given period by its consciousness.

"Just as our opinion of an individual is not based on what he thinks of himself, so can we not judge of such a period of transformation by its consciousness. . . ." [12] More than a society's opinion of itself is necessary in order adequately to comprehend it. Studying various aspects of the social consciousness alone will not yield an understanding either of that consciousness or of that society.

3. To explain the various aspects of a society's consciousness, they must not be treated as autonomous structures enjoying a merely immanent development. Instead, consciousness must be explained in its intimate connection with, and dependence upon, the tension between productive forces and relations of production.

4. Do not expect a revolutionary change of the society so long as the productive forces continue to develop within the existing property relations. Critical interruptions of this development, e.g., crises of "overproduction," are important signals in this respect and suggest that a change in the prevailing system may be imminent.

To be sure, these injunctions, suggestive as they may be, are also very abstract. They pose many problems to the student who would translate them into rigorous research techniques. At the same time they are important general guideposts and essential as a point of departure. In Marx's general approach, the sequence in which the various aspects of the social system must be studied is of primary importance.

He enjoins the student to turn his attention, first of all, to technology. This, the productive activity of men, discloses their mode of dealing with nature. This indispensable process, by which men sustain themselves, forms the social relations among them as well as their mental conceptions. It is in practice a superior strategy, Marx believed, to study the economic foundation of a society and to proceed from there to the "cloudier" realm of ideology. Within the sphere of production, a competent and objective observer can discern the extent to which productive forces are growing or are inhibited by the existing framework of social organization. Associated with the condition of these forces are at least two classes. The workers, or the producers of material goods, stand in a subordinate position because they are non-owners. The conditions under which the productive forces continue to grow are, at the same time, the conditions for the domination of another class, the owners of the means of production. The power of this class is derived from its property ownership, and this invariably finds its *practical* expression in a particular form of the state. The relationship of these two classes is the fundamental one of the system and calls attention to the major locus of conflict, and the potential source of change. The observer must not expect a revolutionary change of the system so long as the workers' struggles have not acquired a political character. Neither should change be expected if the productive forces are not sufficiently developed to provide the requisite technical basis for a new society.

General Approach to the Study of Social Being and Social Consciousness

To illuminate the connection between being and consciousness, Marx postulated a stage in which they constituted a unity. Prior to any division of labor between the material and mental activities of men, their "doing" and their "thinking" were inextricably interwoven. Thus while all human activity had, for example, political, normative, religious, and aesthetic components, these were not yet separate spheres. They were, as Marx says, "the direct efflux of their material behavior." [13] Under these circumstances, there were neither special individuals nor groups that were professional practitioners of politics, law, religion, art, etc. Mental activity was not yet divorced from man's general productive activity and therefore had no autonomous existence. The existing social relations of production between individuals expressed themselves simultaneously as political and legal relations.

A new division of labor changed this state of affairs. Marx described the change in these terms:

. . . these relations [political and legal] are bound to assume an independent existence *vis-à-vis* the individuals. In language, such relations can only be expressed as concepts. The fact that these universals and concepts are accepted as mysterious powers is a necessary consequence of the independent existence assumed by the real relations whose expression they are. Besides this acceptance in everyday consciousness, these universals are also given a special validity and further development by political scientists and jurists who, as a result of the division of labor, are assigned to the cult of these concepts, and who see in them rather than in the relations of production, the true basis of actual property relations.[14]

With this division of labor the separate but interdependent spheres which have come into being are still to be regarded as dependent for their character, change, and development upon the existing relations of production. For example, Marx asserts that the ruling ideas in every age are the ideas of the ruling class. This class, having the means of material production at its disposal, controls also the means of mental production and thereby attempts to impose its ideas upon those who own and control neither. The dominant ideas are nothing more than the mental expressions of the dominant relationships. The ruling class has no need to develop or disseminate these ideas by itself. The division of labor has brought into being a special group of ideologists whose main concern and source of livelihood it is to develop and perfect the illusions of the class about itself and ideologically to defend its interests.

The observer should therefore expect to find a group of professional ideologists who express the interests of the dominant class. At the same time he must not assume a one-to-one relationship between the class and its spokesmen. On the contrary, the development of a cleavage, of hostility, and even opposition, is altogether possible between the two. There are, however, certain objective limits to such a cleavage. In one of his earliest conceptualizations of this problem, Marx asserted that in the event of a collision in which the interests of the class are endangered, the interests would always win out. The cleavage would disappear and with it the illusion that the ruling ideas were not the ideas of the ruling class and had a power distinct from this class.[15]

From the foregoing discussion, it is evident that Marx's theoretical insights may be employed as a general methodological approach. The main point here would be not to reduce everything to economic terms but to disclose the relationship between the economic and non-economic spheres in society.

In order to see how Marx himself employed these general ideas, his journalistic writings will now be examined. In these writings he takes account not only of the capital-labor relation but also of all classes of the society, including "older" classes as well as intermediate strata. Moreover, his attention is not centered on the mode of production; he takes into his purview other spheres of social conduct, e.g., political, legal, etc. The writings considered are: (a) *The Class Struggles in France 1848-1850,* (b) *The 18th Brumaire of Louis Bonaparte,* (c) *Germany: Revolution and Counterrevolution,* and (d) *The Civil War in France.* These works are selected because they are, according to Engels' testimony, Marx's first attempt "to explain a section of contemporary history by means of his materialistic conception, on the basis of the given economic situation." [16] In these works, Marx's method of analysis may be observed concretely as he applies it to the problem of revolution.*

THE CLASS STRUGGLES IN FRANCE

Marx wrote these articles in 1850 and therefore had a short perspective of about 2 years. What was his point of departure? He began his analysis not with the productive forces but with the property relations and from there proceeded to the political aspect. "It was not the French bourgeoisie that ruled under Louis Philippe, but *one* faction of it: bankers, stock exchange kings, railway kings, owners of coal and iron mines and forests, a part of the landed proprietors associated with them—the so-called *finance aristocracy.*" [17] Marx saw as his first task the designation of the class or, more correctly, the particular faction of the class that ruled prior to the struggles of February 1848. The finance aristocracy sat on the throne in the person of Louis Philippe, dictated the laws in the Chambers, and distributed the public offices from Cabinet portfolios to tobacco bureau posts. Clearly, then, a stratum within a class, and not necessarily a class as a whole, can hold power. The scant attention to the economic aspect is expressed simply in the description of the economic spheres in which this stratum was active. Marx then distinguished the other stratum within the class, the *industrial bourgeoisie.* It did not rule, but formed a part of the official opposition and was represented by a minority in the Chambers. In addition, the petty bourgeoisie and the peasantry were excluded from political power as were the *ideological* representatives and spokesmen of the oppositional strata, their savants,

---

* These four works are individually discussed in the four sections immediately following. Parenthetical numbers, following quoted passages, indicate the page of the work from which the quotation was taken.

lawyers, and doctors, etc. Thus the main factions of the bourgeoisie and their respective spokesmen are delineated.

To understand the class structure of the period, however, it was not enough to distinguish the main factions of the bourgeoisie, the industrial and the financial. The role and problems of the former had to be seen in relation to its main antagonist, the working class. Two developments, according to Marx, increased the resoluteness of the industrial bourgeoisie's opposition to the financial aristocracy: First, the growing clarity of the unalloyed rule of the latter; and second, the firm belief of the industrialists that domination of the working class had been secured in the workers' "mutinees of 1832, 1834, and 1839, which had been drowned in blood" (129). The struggle of the industrialists against the financiers was in part carried out by the spokesmen of the former. "Leon Faucher . . . waged a war of the pen for industry against speculation and its train bearer, the government" (129). The struggle of the industrialists was dependent on their relation to the workers. Only after their domination over the workers had been secured could the industrialists increase their opposition to the financiers.

The financial aristocracy that "ruled and legislated through the Chambers had a *direct interest* in the *indebtedness of the state*. The *state deficit* was really the main object of its speculation and the chief source of its enrichment" (129). Here was a faction that profited not from the production of commodities, and the direct extraction of surplus-value from the workers, but from defrauding the state—i.e., from defrauding the opposition classes who paid the taxes to maintain the state budget. The non-ruling factions of the French bourgeoisie cried: Corruption! The industrialists saw their interests endangered, the petty bourgeoisie was filled with moral indignation, and the imagination of the people was offended. Thus Marx based his analysis on classes and sub-classes, their relation to the state and to their ideological representatives. This much was done with only scant reference to economic conditions *per se*. Now he introduced the economic factor by noting that matters had been coming to a head with two international economic events: (a) The potato blight and crop failures of 1845 and 1846, which increased the general ferment among the people, and (b) the general commercial and industrial crisis in

England which hastened the outbreak of the revolution. The after-effect of this crisis had not yet spent itself on the Continent when the February revolution broke out.

Marx attempts to assess the effects of these crises and reviews the sequence of events leading to the uprising: The devastation of trade and industry which made the rule of the finance aristocracy still more unbearable; the growth of the bourgeois opposition agitating throughout France for an electoral reform with which it could win the majority in the Chambers and overthrow the ministry of the Bourse; and, finally, the industrial crisis in Paris itself which threw a "multitude of manufacturers and big traders, who under the existing circumstances could no longer do any business in the foreign market, onto the home market" (133). Their competition with the small storekeepers ruined the latter and their innumerable bankruptcies led them to take revolutionary action in February. Marx relates "how things went as far as hand-to-hand fighting between the people and the army, how the army was disarmed by the passive conduct of the National Guard [the military arm of the bourgeois opposition], how the July monarchy [the political representatives of the financial aristocracy with Louis Philippe as a figurehead] had to give way to a provisional government" (133).

Marx viewed this government as a compromise between the various classes that overthrew the July monarchy. Here the focus is on the dynamics of class relations in a period of rapid political change. No sooner is the provisional government formed when the representatives of the bourgeoisie refuse to proclaim a republic, the declared aim of the revolution. "If Paris, as a result of political centralization, rules France," wrote Marx, then the "workers, in moments of revolutionary earthquakes, rule Paris" (133). This time the workers would hold the bourgeoisie to its word. They would not be deceived again as they were in 1830—when too they fought the battles of the bourgeoisie and instead of a republic were greeted with a monarchy. The workers had manned the barricades then as now and in both uprisings for interests not purely their own. This time (February 1848) they were ready to take up the fight anew and get a republic by force of arms. With this message, Raspail, a leader of the workers, presented himself at the *Hotel de Ville,* the seat of government. In the name of the

Paris proletariat he commanded the government to proclaim a republic. Setting a time limit of two hours, he warned that if this order were not fulfilled he would return at the head of 200,000 men. The time limit had not yet expired when the government acquiesced and proclaimed a republic.

Here Marx's analysis centered on the political aspect, on power. Each class used its power for its own aims. In the case of the industrial bourgeoisie its aim was limited to removing the financial aristocracy and replacing it by its own rule. Even this limited goal was impossible to achieve without enlisting the aid of other classes —the petty bourgeoisie and primarily the Paris proletariat. But the industrial bourgeoisie is faced with a dilemma. It must use the proletariat against the opposition, and at the same time bridle the revolutionary activity of the workers whose aims are less limited and, in fact, those proclaimed by the bourgeoisie at the outset of the struggle—a republic. In Marx's view, then, the revolution reached this stage as a consequence of the pressure of the most radical part of the coalition, the proletariat. The bourgeoisie was forced to make some concessions and the proletariat emerged as an independent party. This, however, was a mixed blessing. For so long as it manned the barricades as a partner in the coalition, there was no open antagonism between the two classes. Having asserted its independence, however, it "challenged the whole of bourgeois France to enter the lists against it" (134). As a result of the revolutionary events, the bourgeoisie acquired political rule. The proletariat, on the other hand, gained only better conditions in which to wage its struggles, i.e., a bourgeois republic.

A ministry of labor was established with no budget and no executive authority, and charged with finding the means of improving the conditions of the working class. The workers thought they could emancipate themselves side by side with the bourgeoisie. This was an illusion. "The development of the industrial proletariat is, in general, conditioned by the development of the industrial bourgeoisie. Only under its rule does the proletariat gain the extensive national existence which can raise its revolution to a national one, and does it itself create the modern means of production which become just so many means of its revolutionary emancipation" (136). But modern industrial relations did not prevail in the whole of France and, as a consequence, neither did the industrial bourgeoisie hold nation-wide power. Its power was confined to Paris and so too was that of the proletariat. In the rest of France, the workers were scattered in small industrial centers and were numerically insignificant compared with the superior numbers of peasants and petty bourgeois. Under these circumstances, the struggle against capital, in its developed, modern form was impossible. It could only remain a partial and local phenomenon.

However, as Marx proceeds in his analysis, he appears to admit the possibility of the workers' taking power even under these conditions, i.e., long before capitalist development has approximated the two-class model. In doing so, he provided a strategy for the underdeveloped areas which was eventually applied by the Bolsheviks. The pre-capitalist, intermediate classes could, under certain conditions, be mobilized by the proletariat, or its leadership, in its behalf. The revolution could not succeed, Marx believed, until "it had aroused the mass of the nation, peasants and petty bourgeoisie, against this order, against the rule of capital, and had forced it to attach itself to the proletarians as their protagonists" (137). This revolutionary prerequisite was not present during this period. It is a justifiable inference, however, on the basis of the quoted statement, that the requisite conditions could present themselves long before capitalist development had attained the advanced stage in which Marx typically expected a workers' revolution.

Marx described some of the factors that arrested the revolution at this stage and which were not at all inevitable. The financial aristocracy, the same group that was to be dislodged by the revolution, forced the provisional government into a growing deficit. The industrial-bourgeoisie Marx argued, could have nationalized the banks long before the government fell into such straits. But to do so would only encourage the workers to go even further. On the contrary, the main task of the bourgeois factions had now become to oppose not the finance aristocracy but the workers—to hold the latter in check. The weapon employed against them was a new tax.

The new tax, and upon whom it was imposed, revealed to Marx the character of the government. The tax was the wedge which had to be driven between the proletariat and its potential allies if the revolution was to be arrested at this stage of its development. Who was taxed? "The Bourse wolves, the bank kings, the state creditors, the *rentiers,* the industrialists? That was not the way to ingratiate the republic with the bourgeoisie . . . . But someone had to fork out the cash. Who was sacrificed to bourgeois credit? Jacques le Bonhomme, the peasant" (141). The Paris proletariat was cajoled into believing that the tax would fall only on the big landed proprietors. In fact, it hit the peasant class, the large majority of the French people, and in them gained the social basis for counterrevolution. The tax was a question of life and death for the peasant. From the moment it was imposed, the "republic meant to the French peasant the 45 centimes tax, *and he saw in the Paris proletariat the spendthrift who did himself well at his expense"* (141). Thus in his analysis of a relatively complicated state of affairs, Marx used economic variables with an eye to their political implications and the relations among the classes.

The revolution had a different meaning for each of the various classes and strata. Each had its own interests and its own aims. The industrial bourgeoisie, to attain its limited aims, had to enlist the classes "below" it; the latter had to subordinate their aims to those of the bourgeoisie. To push the revolution beyond the bourgeois stage, certain objective conditions, i.e., nation-wide industrial relations of production, had to prevail. In the absence of these conditions there was still an alternative, viz., the enlistment of the intermediate classes to the side of the proletariat. This was possible only with the awareness on the part of those classes that their interests and those of the proletariat coincided, if only temporarily. This coalition of lower classes might have taken place, Marx believed, had the imposition of the new tax been seen by the peasants for what it was—a measure used against them by the bourgeois government in order not to estrange the bourgeoisie. Instead, the peasants blamed the proletariat and a wedge was successfully driven between them and the workers. Pushing the revolution forward was impossible so long as they remained divided. But neither was the revolution at a standstill.

For Marx the February republic had revealed itself as a bourgeois republic. Yet it was won with the active support of the workers and only the passive support of the bourgeoisie.

The proletarians rightly regarded themselves as the victors of February and they made the arrogant claims of victors. They had to be vanquished in the streets, they had to be shown that they were worsted as soon as they did not fight *with* the bourgeoisie, but *against* the bourgeoisie. Just as the February republic, with its socialist concessions, required a battle of the proletariat, united with the bourgeoisie, against the monarchy, so a second battle was necessary to sever the republic from the socialist concessions, in order to officially work out the *bourgeois republic* as dominant (146-147).

This occurred not with the February victory but with the June defeat. It could be accomplished only by dividing the proletariat against itself and by provoking it to insurrection not on its own terms but at the initiative of the bourgeoisie. Marx proceeded to describe the tactics of the bourgeoisie which in some respects foreshadowed those of 20th-century fascism. The provisional government organized the *lumpenproletariat* and brought it to its side. These were a mass sharply differentiated from the industrial workers, and not a proletariat at all. Thieves and criminals of all kinds, they were capable of the "basest banditry and the foulest corruption" (142). At the same time a vast army of unemployed was organized. "A hundred thousand workers, thrown on the streets by the crisis and the revolution, were enrolled in so-called *ateliers*" (143). These were English workhouses in the open at which the workers were employed at unproductive, tedious and monotonous earthworks. In addition, the government issued a series of provocative decrees prohibiting the congregation of people, making the admission to the *ateliers* more difficult, introducing a piece wage, and banishing the unemployed workers from Paris. Finally, the government "ordered the forcible expulsion of all unmarried workers from the national *ateliers* or their enrollment in the army" (147). "The workers were left no choice; they had to starve or let fly. They answered on June 22 [1848] with the tremendous insurrection in which the first great battle was fought between the two classes that split modern society. It was a fight for the preservation or annihilation of the *bourgeois* order" (147). The fight ended with the defeat of the workers, the so-called *June* defeat, which was inflicted with "unheard of brutality," and the "massacring [of] over 3,000 prisoners" (147). This chain of events provided Marx with the evidence that on the Continent significant improvement in the position of the workers remains a *"utopia within* the bourgeois republic, a utopia that becomes a crime as soon as it wants to become a reality" (149). On the basis of these events, Marx formed the opinion that where such conditions prevail, force may be necessary to effect any revolutionary change in the society. It was precisely during these years (1848-1852) that Marx put forward with greater resoluteness what he called the "bold slogan of revolutionary struggle: *Overthrow of the bourgeoisie:* Dictatorship of the working class!" (149).

In Marx's analysis of the role of the intermediate classes in the revolution, he emphasized their vacillatory character. Though the peasantry could have gone either way, i.e., with the workers or with the bourgeoisie, depending on the conditions, in the prevailing circumstances it went over to the bourgeoisie. The other important intermediate class, the petty bourgeoisie,

> . . . marched against the barricades in order to restore the traffic which leads from the streets into the shop. But behind the barricade stood the customers and the debtors; before it the creditors of the shop. And when the barricades were thrown down and the workers were crushed and the shopkeepers, drunk with victory, rushed back to their shops, they found the entrance barred by a savior of property, and official agent of credit, who presented them with threatening notices: Overdue promissory note! Overdue house rent! Overdue bond! Doomed Shop! Doomed Shopkeeper! (153).

By striking down the workers the shopkeepers had delivered themselves into the hands of their creditors.

In this article, as later in the *18th Brumaire of Louis Bonaparte,* an important part of Marx's analysis rests on the role of the "great man," in history and his relation with the various classes. The bourgeoisie, to consolidate its gains while accepting the republic, attempted to legitimize its rule through election. It is here that Louis Napoleon, the "nephew of the uncle," made his appearance with far-reaching consequences for all classes of French society. In December of 1848, he was elected president of the republic and it was primarily the peasants who elected him. The republic, it will be recalled, had announced itself to the peasants with the tax collector; they, in turn, announced themselves to the republic with Napoleon. Here was the man who represented the interests of the peasants, but only in their imagination. For them the memory of the "uncle" was still alive and they marched to the polls shouting: "No more taxes, down with the rich, down with the republic, long live the emperor!" (159). For Marx, however, this was the nephew and not the uncle, not a "great man" but a caricature of one. "The most simple-minded man in France acquired the most multifarious significance. Just because he was nothing, he could signify everything save himself" (160).

The name Napoleon had a specific and different meaning for each of the classes. It was not yet the *man* Louis Napoleon who had these various effects on the development of the revolution, but his *name*. Here in his concrete analysis of actual events—the impression of his theoretical writings notwithstanding—it can be seen that for Marx *imagination* and *ideas* were not mere epiphenomena. The respective classes imagined that Louis Napoleon personified their interests. They were wrong, and what they imagined was "false consciousness." This false consciousness, far from having no effect, had a profound one on the various classes. It obscured their objective interests (which Marx imputed to each class) and in the case of the workers, for example, prevented them from acting in their own best interests.

What was the meaning of the name Napoleon to the other classes beside the peasantry? To the workers it meant the overthrow of those who inflicted the June defeat upon them. The petty bourgeoisie hopefully interpreted it as the rule of the debtors over the creditors. For the majority within the big bourgeoisie the election of Napoleon meant an open breach with the petty bourgeoisie, the faction whose support was needed against the revolution, "but which became intolerable to it as soon as this faction sought to consolidate the position of the moment into a constitutional position" (160).

While the majority of both the petty bourgeoisie and the proletariat supported the great name, the more advanced sections of these classes put forward their own candidates. For the advanced section of the proletariat, for example, it was a protest vote—against the trend the republic had taken. Thus Marx saw a small segment of the proletariat attempting to separate itself from the bourgeois parties and constitute itself as an independent party. This segment was developing "true consciousness." The petty bourgeoisie, on the other hand, and its parliamentary representative, the Montagne, treated their candidates "with all the seriousness with which it is in the habit of solemnly duping itself" (160). Both classes were beaten on December 10, 1848 with the election of the nephew. And Marx observed: "France now possessed a Napoleon side by side with a *Montagne,* proof that both were only the lifeless caricatures of the great realities whose names they bore" (160). Marx set himself the task of explaining the conditions which led first to the election and then to the *coup d'état* of Louis Bonaparte on December 2, 1851.

THE 18TH BRUMAIRE OF LOUIS BONAPARTE

Marx opened his discussion by observing that now with a second Napoleon and a second "mountain" a people "which had imagined that by means of a revolution it had imparted to itself an accelerated power of motion, suddenly finds itself set back into a defunct epoch . . ." (226). In reviewing the events that led to the *coup d'état,* Marx saw three main periods.

The first he called the prologue to the revolution. Louis Philippe was deposed and the character of the period was officially expressed in the *provisional* government. It was provisional in that everything it attempted and enunciated turned out to be only provisional. "All the elements that had prepared or determined the revolution, the dynastic opposition, the republican bourgeoisie, and democratic-republican petty bourgeoisie and the social-democratic workers, provisionally found their place in the February *government*" (230). In Marx's view, it could not have been otherwise. The bourgeois opposition, in the February days, had as its main aim widening the circle of politically privileged within the possessing class itself, and accomplished this. Each participating class, however, construed the revolution in its own way. The proletariat, for example, participating arms in hand, impressed its stamp upon it and proclaimed it a *social* republic, i.e., aimed at its social amelioration. It had not realized that its aims were "in most singular contradiction to everything that with the material available, with the degree of education attained by the masses, under the given circumstances and relations, could be immediately realized in practice" (230). On the other hand, the claims of all the remaining elements that had cooperated in the February revolution were recognized by the share they had obtained in the government. It was a period of confusion, of a temporary coalition of classes each with its own aims and all working at cross purposes; some strove for change and others for the continuation of the old routine. The bourgeois opposition mobilized the proletariat in its behalf and found support also in the peasants and petty bourgeois, who entered the political stage with their own demands after the July monarchy, the exclusive rule of the financial aristocracy, had fallen.

The second period was that of the foundation of the bourgeois republic. The industrial bourgeoisie now had to achieve a double purpose. It aimed at limiting the power of the financiers by increasing its own, an impossible task without the support of the classes below it. Simultaneously, it had to put an end to the pretensions of the workers and confine the revolution to its bourgeois limits. When the proletariat recognized this fact and attempted to act in its own behalf, its demands were branded as utopian nonsense. The Paris proletariat replied with the *June insurrection,* and was crushed. The bourgeois republic had triumphed. On its side stood the financial aristocracy, the industrial bourgeoisie, the middle class, the army, the *lumpenproletariat,* the professional intellectuals, the clergy and the rural population. On the other side stood the proletariat alone. The third period began with the election of Louis Napoleon in December of 1848 and culminated in his seizure of power in December 1851.

In curbing the classes below it, Marx argued, the bourgeoisie had paved the way for its own decline. Not only the pressures of the proletariat, but also the demands of the petty bourgeoisie and their efforts at retaining the republic, had to be cut short. Having lost all support from the classes below it, no one remained to defend the bourgeoisie against the unchecked executive power as represented by Louis Bonaparte. France therefore seemed "to have escaped the despotism of a class only to fall back beneath the despotism of an individual. . . ." The struggle appeared "to be settled in such a way that all classes, equally impotent and equally mute, fell on their knees before the rifle butt" (300). It was only an illusion, however, that the state had made itself completely independent. For the "state power is not suspended in midair. Bonaparte represents a class, and the most numerous class of French society at that, the *small holding peasants*" (302). Both the election of Bonaparte in December of 1848 and his *coup d'état* of December 1851 rested on this social basis. In his discussion of the peasantry, Marx's conception of "class" becomes clearer. He distinguished its objective and subjective aspects.

The small-holding peasants form a vast mass, the members of which live in similar conditions but without entering into manifold relations with one another. Their mode of production isolates them from one another instead of bringing them into mutual intercourse . . . . In this way, the great mass of the French nation is formed by a simple addition of homologous magnitudes, much as potatoes in a sack form a sack of potatoes. In so far as millions of families live under economic conditions of existence that separate their mode of life, their interests and their culture from those of the other classes, and put them in hostile opposition to the latter, *they form a class.* In so far as there is merely a local interconnection among these small-holding peasants, and the identity of their interests begets no community, no national bond and no political organization among them, *they do not form a class* (Italics mine.) (303).

Objectively the peasants are a class; subjectively they are not. Unable to represent themselves, their political influence finds its expression in the executive power, Louis Bonaparte.

But matters are even more complicated. Marx saw Louis Napoleon's power resting not on the peasant class as a whole, but on its conservative as against its revolutionary strata. Bonaparte represented not the peasant that

. . . strikes out beyond the condition of his social existence, the small holding, but rather the peasant who wants to consolidate this holding, not the country folk who, linked up with the towns, want to overthrow the old order through their own energies, but on the contrary those who, in stupefied seclusion within this old order, want to see themselves and their small holdings saved . . . . It represents not the enlightenment, but the superstition of the peasant; not his judgment but his prejudice; not his future but his past . . ." (303-304).

This struggle between the "backward" and "forward" looking consciousness of the peasantry was not carried out in an abstract Hegelian fashion. It took the form of a continual struggle between schoolmasters and priests. The bourgeoisie, fearful of the peasantry's enlightenment, suppressed the schoolmasters. When the more advanced strata of the peasantry tried to act independently in the face of the bourgeois government by choosing their own local representatives, the latter were also suppressed. Finally, when the peasants in some localities rose against the army, they were punished with states of siege and suppressed. The bourgeoisie and its government feared "the stupidity of the masses as long as they remained conservative, and the insight of the masses as soon as they became revolutionary" (304).

For Marx, the class situation provided the key to Bonaparte's power. Though not suspended in midair, his power rested on an unfirm basis. For while the executive authority had become a somewhat independent power, its main function was to safeguard the "bourgeois order." The executive took from the bourgeoisie its political power but left untouched its economic power. By protecting the latter, Bonaparte generated its political power anew. Bonaparte *appeared* as the benefactor of all classes but could give to one class only by taking from another. He ruled by the contradictory demands of his situation—indeed, it was this situation that made his rule possible. These were some of the contradictory aspects of the situation which Marx observed.

To summarize, the first thing that becomes clear from Marx's analysis is that he assigned enormous importance to the *political* events taking place at the time. This was his primary focus and only intermittently did he draw attention to the economic conditions allegedly underlying them. In a letter to Conrad Schmidt, Engels asserts that this was in fact Marx's intention. "If therefore [anyone] supposes that we deny any and every reaction, of the political, etc., reflexes of the economic movement upon the movement itself, he is simply tilting at windmills. He has only to look at Marx's *Eighteenth Brumaire,* which deals almost exclusively with the *particular* part played by political struggles and events, of course within their general dependence upon economic conditions." [18] This is what Marx attempted in these writings. But his attempt, as we shall see, was accompanied by great methodological difficulties. For no sooner does Engels assert that seeking after the economic conditions is necessary, than he denies that it is possible. If events "are judged by current history, *it will never be possible* to go back to the ultimate economic causes." [19] This is due, in Engels' opinion, to the complexity of economic changes. Even where there is an abundance of information on economic affairs and changes, it is impossible to follow the daily movement of industry and trade. These complicated and ever-changing factors create additional difficulties because they are often not perceptible until they make themselves felt. Engels concludes therefore that, "A clear survey of the economic history of a given period can never be obtained contemporaneously but only subsequently after a collecting and sifting of the material has taken place." [20] How did Marx cope with these difficulties? He treated the economic situation as relatively constant for the period under consideration. Engels adequately described Marx's approach when he wrote that in employing it one must limit oneself ". . . to tracing political conflicts back to the struggles between the interests of the existing social classes and fractions of classes created by the economic development, and to prove the particular political parties to be the more or less adequate political expression of these same classes and fractions of classes." [21]

On the basis of Marx's analysis in the two articles considered, at least the following procedural steps can be made explicit:

(a) Obtain a general overview of the economic process of a specific period; note its main trends and direction of change.

(b) Hold this economic situation constant.

(c) Isolate for observation all classes and fractions of classes and determine their respective objective interests.

(d) Locate the political parties of the period.

(e) Link the parties to the classes and determine the degree to which the former express the interests of the latter.

This is what Marx attempted to do, and within the limits of the difficulties described, he believed he had succeeded in explaining the events from 1848 to 1851. He concluded this on the basis of two tests which he himself applied. The first was in 1850 when he reviewed the economic history of the previous decade and concluded that the world trade crisis of 1847 was the precondition for the revolution and that the industrial prosperity, that had become evident since the middle of 1848, was the revitalizing force of the counterrevolution. The second test consisted of his review of economic events from 1848 to December of 1851 which he worked out after the *coup d'état,* and where he found that he had very little to change. Marx was satisfied that his theory had given him sufficient guidance in his interpretation of the recent past.

While Marx may have been right about the connection he imputed to economic and political events of the recent past, he was wrong about the importance of a new crisis. He wrote in 1850: "A new revolution is possible only in the wake of a new crisis. It is, however, just as certain as this crisis." [22] Throughout this period he and Engels were confident that given a new crisis, the revolution would continue to develop until it culminated in the elimination of capitalist relations. "History has proved us, and all who thought like us wrong," Engels admitted years later. "It has made it clear that the state of economic development on the continent at that time was not, by a long way, ripe for the elimination of capitalist production." [23] Thus Marx's theoretical approach enabled him to explain the past but failed him in his predictions. His method was encumbered with difficulties which are inherent in any attempt to comprehend a whole society in the process of rapid change. Before deciding whether these difficulties are insuperable, the approach must be examined further.

GERMANY: REVOLUTION AND COUNTERREVOLUTION[24]

In 1851, when the failure of the revolution on the continent had become clear, Engels wrote: "Everyone knows nowadays that whenever there is a revolutionary convulsion, there must be some social want in the background, which is prevented by outworn institutions from satisfying itself. The want may not be felt as strongly, as generally, as might ensure immediate success, but every attempt at forcible repression will only bring it forth stronger and stronger, until it bursts its fetters." [25] For Engels these are the conditions that make for social change: The tension between changing and/or growing social wants on the one hand, and their frustration by incompatible social institutions on the other. This proposition, however, is at a very high level of generalization. Revolutions took place in innumerable places and countries in the middle of the 19th century and no single generalization could cover them all without losing a great deal of information. This is not to imply that Marx was not interested in generalizations about societies in general. Many of his theoretical propositions he considered applicable to *all* class societies and *all* capitalist societies as working hypotheses, of course, and not dogmatic assertions. Moreover, as we have seen, Marx had adumbrated a plan of study in which he proposed to study the abstract characteristics common to societies in general. Though Marx never accomplished this with respect to *all* forms of society it is clear that he was moving in that direction in his study of capitalism. In *Capital* he was clearly describing the abstract characteristics common to all capitalist societies. In addition, he did considerable work on pre-capitalist societies. But Marx believed that the way to build general theory is to study first the particular conditions of the society in question. In the case of revolution, for example, each situation must be studied afresh. Marx would never have considered it adequate to explain a particular revolution as the result of the tension between "productive forces" and "relations of production," and leave it at that. For Marx, this would have been mere phrase mongering; and he had nothing but contempt for those who turned everything into a phrase in order to cover up their scanty historical knowledge and fit it into a neat system as quickly as possible. In contrast, Marx fastidiously studied each individual case and only then drew general conclusions. To understand revolution as a social phenomenon, the causes must be sought in the "conditions of existence of each of the convulsed nations." [26] What is suggested then, is that Marx and Engels employed a comparative method in which they carefully considered the varying conditions of different places and different periods.

It has been seen in the works previously considered that Marx used as his main working concepts, classes, strata, parties, etc. In these writings, the countries in question were not simply defined as capitalist and left at that. The prevalence of capitalist industrial relations, the existence of older and intermediate classes, the international relations of the country concerned, etc., are all treated by Marx as empirical problems. Never, when referring to two societies as capitalist, did he assume that sharing this system of production makes for identical consequences. All generalizations about capitalist systems were qualified by considering the specific social conditions of the society in question.

In this approach one centers his attention not only on general forms but on particular forms as well; not only are the forms common to all societies, or all societies of a certain type, taken into purview, but also the combination of forms peculiar to individual societies during certain definite periods. It is a comparative method but something more than this. It urges one to view social structures in definite historical contexts. The logic of the method works in something like the following terms: Similar structures and tendencies are observed in a number of societies and it is decided that it may be useful to classify them as societies of a certain type—e.g., capitalist-industrial. By abstracting the common characteristics from the various societies, and pulling them together into a general working model of this type of society, one can generate hypotheses about the elements of the model and the interrelationship among them. For instance, in virtually all modern industrial societies it is observed that lower, disadvantaged strata vote for more radical, left-wing parties, while upper, privileged strata vote for more conservative, right-wing parties. Having made this generalization, it must be asked, Do these relationships obtain under all circumstances and in all periods? Where and when does it not hold true? Finding that the generalization does not apply in a given case, the answer must be sought not only in the functional relationship of the elements of the system but in the history of the system and its component elements as well. For example, as was seen earlier, Marx and Engels developed their general theory of change—using the key concepts *productive forces* and *property relations*—in a specific historical context. They then employed it as a general working hypothesis in their studies of the various societies of their time. Certain revolutions took place (in 1848); some succeeded only partially and others failed altogether. Why did revolutions succeed in one place and fail in another? The general theory is not sufficient to explain either. In one place the productive forces break through and succeed, at least partially, in changing the power relations. In another place the productive forces fail to do so because the existing relations are too rigid. The latter situation was the concrete historical case that Engels wanted to understand—the failure of the revolution in Germany. To explain this failure, a careful investigation of the specific circumstances of Germany, in the period in question, had to be undertaken. But it was not enough to confine attention to that period. One had to go sufficiently back in time to see the origin of the conditions in question. In Engels' view, then, one must take account of social structure *and* history—not just social structure. This methodological injunction was emphasized in another connection by Joseph Schumpeter: "No decade in the history of politics, religion, technology, painting, poetry and whatnot ever contains its own explanation. In order to understand the events [of various given periods] . . . you must survey a period of much wider span. Not to do so is the hallmark of dilettantism." [27] In Engels' analysis of the revolution and its defeat in Germany, the importance of this principle of analysis is clearly borne out.

Engels begins with a description of the class-structure in Germany which was quite different from that of England and France.

> The composition of the different classes of the people which form the groundwork of every political organization was, in Germany, more complicated than in any other country. While in England and France feudalism was entirely destroyed, or at least reduced, as in the former country, to a few insignificant forms by a powerful and wealthy middle class, concentrated in large towns, . . . the feudal nobility in Germany had retained a great portion of their ancient privileges.[28]

Thus beginning with a specific condition peculiar to Germany in that period, he emphasized the power of the feudal lords. The condition of the bourgeoisie was also different in Germany. It was neither as wealthy nor as concentrated as its opposite number in France and England. The old manufactures of Germany had been destroyed by the introduction of steam and the severe competition and supremacy of English manufactures. "The more modern manufactures . . . [in Germany] did not compensate for the loss of the old ones, nor suffice to create a manufacturing interest strong enough to force its wants upon the notice of governments jealous of every extension of non-noble wealth and power." [29] Engels saw a relative "backwardness" in German capitalist development and sought to explain it in terms of the specific historical experiences of Germany. "The causes of this backwardness of German manufactures were manifold, but two will suffice to account for it: the unfavorable geographic situation of the country, at a distance from the Atlantic, which had become the great highway for the world's trade; and the continuous wars in which Germany was involved, and which were fought on her soil, from

the sixteenth century to the present day." [30] The reader should
not be misled by the word "geographical" in this context. Engels'
meaning here has nothing in common with geographical determinism. In this context the term refers to the historical circumstances
that accelerated the economic development of those countries on
the Atlantic seaboard and retarded the development of those
separated from the great highways of trade. These historically
specific conditions made for a weak bourgeoisie in Germany. It
was small in number and not concentrated in any significant degree
and this prevented it from attaining the political supremacy that
the English bourgeoisie achieved in 1688 and the French in 1789.
Here the correlative growth which Engels saw in the economic and
political development of a class is clear. He explains the political
weakness of the German bourgeoisie by its weak economic development.

However, even this weak bourgeoisie was growing in economic
importance, particularly from 1815, and consequently also in
political importance. Engels provides a very specific and concrete
example of developing productive forces coming into conflict with
existing relations of production. The growing bourgeoisie "soon
arrived at a stage where it found the development of its most important interests checked by the political constitution of the country—by its random division among thirty-six princes with conflicting tendencies and caprices; by the feudal fetters upon agriculture
and the trade connected with it; by the prying superintendence to
which an ignorant and presumptuous bureaucracy subjected all
its transactions." [31]

What about the other classes in Germany at the time? As in the
case of the nobility and bourgeoisie, the petty bourgeoisie also
differed from its counterpart in other countries, e.g., England and
France. The small trading and shopkeeping class was exceedingly
numerous in Germany owing to the lagging development of the
large capitalists there. If the petty bourgeoisie played such an important role in determining the outcome of other revolutions—
owing to its intermediate position and its consequent vacillatory
character—then all the more so in the case of Germany. In Germany this class was directly dependent on the monarchy and the
aristocracy. It was "eternally tossed about between the hope of

entering the ranks of the wealthier class and the fear of being reduced to the state of proletarians or even paupers . . . ." [32]

What was the condition of the German working class? If large-scale industry was undeveloped could the working class be anything else? "In Germany, the mass of the working class were employed, not by those modern manufacturing lords of which Great Britain furnishes such splendid specimens, but by small tradesmen whose entire manufacturing system is a mere relic of the middle ages." [33] Thus far Engels has been considering mainly the *foundation,* the totality of productive relations constituting the economic structure of society. What about the *superstructure?* It too was historically specific owing to its correlative development with the foundation. The general absence of modern conditions of production, transportation and communication was accompanied by the absence of modern ideas. "It is therefore not to be wondered at if, at the outbreak of the revolution, a large part of the working classes should cry out for the immediate re-establishment of guilds and medieval privileged trades' corporations." [34] Yet, this class was not of a piece. Some workers lived and worked in the few factory districts that did exist and where large-scale production was the dominant form. These workers, according to Engels, had a clearer conception of their life conditions.

Finally, Engels considered the large class of farmers and the extent of its stratification. First, there were wealthy farmers who owned extensive farms and employed several laborers. This stratum was located between the large untaxed feudal land owners and the smaller peasantry, and allied itself with the anti-feudal middle class of the towns. Secondly, there were the small freeholders of the Rhine area who benefited from the influence of the Great French Revolution and its destruction of feudalism there; similar "free-holders" existed in other provinces but were free in name only, their plots being heavily mortgaged. Thirdly, there were the feudal tenants and, finally, the agricultural laborers who "lived and died poor, and ill-fed." In Engels' view, the freeholders, the tenants and the agricultural laborers stood to gain the most from the revolution. However, these would not or perhaps could not move on their own initiative. Dispersed over a great space with no communication among a sufficient number of them, they could never initiate an independent movement. They required the impulse of the more concentrated and more educated people of the towns. Thus this survey of the specific class structure of Germany, and the varied and conflicting interests of the classes, was employed by Engels to explain the high degree of confusion that reigned during the revolution and its resulting failure.

In the further development of his analysis, Engels painstakingly considered each area in Germany and the role of the various classes within it. For example, he carefully scrutinized the specific conditions of the Prussian state, the other German states, Austria, the Vienna insurrection, the Berlin insurrection, etc. In addition, he considered outside influences, particularly French, upon the course of events in Germany. The German bourgeoisie after its own uprising, sensing that it could not hold its ground against the feudal and bureaucratic parties without popular support, tried to mobilize the latter. The German bourgeoisie, however, was more fearful of the masses below than of the feudal powers above and in this respect was quite similar to its counterpart in Paris. It made only limited demands upon the feudal parties and the latter made even more limited concessions. The German bourgeoisie soon accepted these concessions so that together with the feudal parties it could cut short the demands of the more radical parties. After the defeat of the Parisian workers in June of 1848, when it became clear that the Paris revolution had been crushed, the old feudal bureaucratic party in Germany decided to rid itself even of its momentary ally, the German bourgeoisie, and to restore Germany to the *status quo ante*. In his 19th letter, in which he described the close of the insurrection, Engels wrote these prophetic words, the result of a historically specific analysis: "Political liberalism, the rule of the bourgeoisie, be it under a monarchical or republican form of government, is forever impossible in Germany." [35]

THE CIVIL WAR IN FRANCE [36]

Marx and Engels believed that in France, after 1789, no revolution could break out without having, at least in part, a proletarian character. In each of the revolutions since then—1830, 1848 and, finally, the Paris Commune in 1871—they viewed the proletariat as the really radical element enlisted by the bourgeoisie to attain its own limited aims and, having achieved them, turned upon the workers and thrust them back. In general terms they saw in these revolutions that after the first great success the revolutionary partners divided. One half was satisfied with what had been gained, the other wanted to go still further and put forward new demands. The first victory was possible only with the participation of the more radical party. With this victory, however, the radicals became expendable and even the main enemy. In each of the French revolutions the proletariat advanced its own demands but these were unclear and confused. The demands corresponded to the state of development reached by the workers of Paris at the particular period. With all their lack of clarity and confusion these still constituted a "threat to the existing order of society; the workers who put them forward were still armed; therefore, the disarming of the workers was the first commandment of the bourgeois, who were at the helm of the state. Hence, after every revolution won by the workers, a new struggle, ending with the defeat of the workers." [37]

If the proletariat was unable to make its revolution and rule France, neither could the bourgeoisie. For it, too, had not yet reached the necessary stage of its development, divided as it was into conflicting strata and parties. It was this lack of unity, itself a consequence of the absence of the domination of modern industrial relations throughout France, which Marx saw as the condition which allowed Louis Bonaparte to gain control of the state and all its command posts—the army, the police and the bureaucracy. Despite this rule of a "gang of political and financial adventurers," France underwent an industrial development which had been impossible under previous regimes, e.g., that of the financial aristocracy and Louis Philippe. Thus in spite of the apparently simultaneous anti-bourgeois, anti-proletarian character of Bonaparte's rule, it served, in Marx's view, the interests of the further development of the productive forces and the capitalist mode of production.

At the same time, the Second Empire, under Louis Napoleon, was "the appeal to French chauvinism, was the demand for the restoration of the frontiers of the First Empire which had been lost in 1814, or at least those of the First Republic." [38] This led, in 1870, to the Franco-Prussian war which drove Louis Napoleon first to Sedan and from there to Wilhemsrohe. The French army was defeated and the Emperor interned. While the war still raged, the workers of Paris rose up once again, the empire collapsed, and the republic was again proclaimed. At first the workers allowed the former legislative body to form a government of defense. But soon the antagonism between the bourgeois government and the armed workers broke into open conflict. Finally, when Paris capitulated —and this greatly impressed Marx and Engels—the Prussian army did not dare enter Paris in triumph. It occupied only a small corner of Paris while being itself encircled by the Paris proletariat "who kept a sharp watch that no 'Prussian' should overstep the narrow bounds of the corner ceded to the foreign conqueror." [39] After the repeated attempts of the bourgeois government to topple the new workers' government, the latter was finally established. This was the Paris Commune. The workers, having taken power in Paris, embarked immediately upon a remarkable policy. They abolished conscription and the army, decreed the separation of church from state, remitted all payments of rent for a certain period, and elected foreigners to office as a sign of the international character of the Commune. All officials were paid salaries not exceeding that of a worker's average wage and the Commune attempted immediately to establish its egalitarian character—and all the while fighting a war of survival against the "armies assembled by the Versailles [bourgeois] government in ever-growing numbers." [40] Further developments revealed to Marx the internationalism of the bourgeoisie as well as of the proletariat.

The government of Versailles, the same that had prosecuted the war against Prussia, now confronted with the Commune, turned to the enemy and "begged the Prussian government for the hasty return of the French soldiers taken prisoner at Sedan and Metz, in order that they may recapture Paris for them." [41] The Commune was crushed. This historical experience confirmed the conclusions which Marx had begun to reach 20 years earlier. The working class, having taken power, could not go on managing with the old state organization. It must, on the one hand, "do away with all the repressive machinery previously used against itself, and, on the other, safeguard itself against its own deputies and officials, by declaring them all, without exception, subject to recall at any moment." [42]

Thus in addition to classes, sub-classes and parties, the problem of bureaucracy became increasingly important in Marx's analysis from the time of the 18th Brumaire to that of the Commune. He definitely anticipated the role of bureaucratic organization in inhibiting the growth of democracy to which Weber and afterwards Michels, gave so much attention. The following passage from Engels' introduction to *Civil War in France* is almost a verbatim anticipation of Michels' thesis on the "iron law of oligarchy."

> Society had created its own organs to look after its common interests, originally through simple division of labor. But these organs, at whose head was the state power, had in the course of time, in pursuance of their own special interests, transformed themselves from servants of society into masters of society.[43]

For Marx, however, this characteristic of bureaucracy prevailed only under certain conditions, and was in no sense inevitable under all social conditions. It was neither a basis for pessimism as with Weber nor an "iron law" as with Michels. For Marx the transformation of the bureaucratic organs of the state from servants to masters of society could be prevented by two infallible means, those in fact employed by the Commune. "It filled all posts—administrative, judicial and educational—by election on the basis of universal suffrage of all concerned, subject to the right of recall at any time by the same electors. And, in the second place, all officials, high or low, were paid only the wages received by other workers . . . . In this way an effective barrier to place-hunting and careerism was set up, even apart from the binding mandates to delegates to representative bodies which were added besides." [44] Clearly, then, Marx and Engels were aware of the problems of bureaucracy and pointed out some of the means by which its anti-democratic effects could be eliminated or at least mitigated.

This survey of selected writings by Marx and Engels provides a clearer understanding of the way they employed their theory as a guide to social analysis. They were guided by an implicit paradigm for social analysis and it is our task in the next section to make it explicit.

MARX'S PARADIGM FOR AN ANALYSIS OF THE STRUCTURE
AND CHANGE OF WHOLE SOCIETIES

The student of society should study first the mode of production of the society in question. This means that attention is first turned to the following four factors which are all to be regarded as causally active:

(a) The direct producers in their cooperative "work-relations" and the technological know-how with which they carry on the labor process.

(b) The instruments and means of production.

(c) The property relations governing access to and control of the means of production and its products.

(d) Nature, and the way it conditions the productive process.

Nowhere does Marx assert which of these factors is the universally decisive one determining the various forms of society and consequently, the different kinds of people within them. All that the student can be sure of, prior to investigation, is that every society will integrate, in its own distinctive way, purposive labor, its social organization, its means of production and its natural basis. It is a matter of empirical investigation which of these will be the dominant factor in any particular case. Thus to understand "present day industrial society," for example, we study the particular form of integration assumed by these factors in a number of industrial societies and construct a tentative model on that basis. To understand why any given industrial society does not conform to the model, we study its specific conditions. Moving back and forth between the general and particular, and accordingly modifying the former, we formulate generalizations about industrial society in general. With these procedural guides in mind, a checklist of the factors Marx took into account, and the approximate sequence in which he considered them, can be presented. In presenting these factors, comments are made suggesting adaptations of Marx's conceptual apparatus for present-day social research.

1. Consider first the economic order and, within it, the sphere of production of the society in question. Beginning with a definite

base line in time, observe the main changes taking place. Even if the student cannot keep apace of the minute, day by day changes, he can observe the main structural changes within this sphere. For example, in present-day industrial society the effects of automation, even in its early stages, can be observed in the following: (a) changing "work-relations," (b) the numerical decline of production workers, (c) the changing structure of the new middle class, and (d) changes in the effectiveness and structure of unions. Questions such as the following would also have to constitute a central focus from this point of view. How does the new technology affect the level of production? Is unemployment rising or declining? To what extent is the change a nation-wide or merely local phenomenon? Although these questions are extremely complex, relevant data is much more timely, plentiful and refined today than in Marx's time. For this reason it is not necessary to hold the economic situation "constant" for periods as long as Marx did. Economic data are perhaps less a source of error today than a century ago.

2. Locate the main classes in the economic structure. Determine the role of each in the processes of production, distribution, and exchange. Locate also the various sub-classes or strata in the economic structure.

3. The informed observer should be able to determine the objective economic interests of the respective classes and strata. Toward this end questions such as the following could be asked: Do the direct producers own or control the tools and other means of production? If not, who does own and/or control them? Does there exist an economic surplus of material goods over and above the subsistence requirements of the producers? Who has control of the surplus? How is it used and which classes benefit most directly from it?

4. Are class-members aware of their objective position in the economic structure and the extent to which it determines their "life chances?" One indicator of this awareness is the conflict among the classes in the economic sphere. A better indicator of class consciousness is the degree to which it finds *political* expression.

5. What form does conflict take among the classes? Within the classes?

6. What is the role of the *lumpenproletariat?* How does its existence affect the other classes? Which classes exploit its existence for their own political ends?

7. Where political parties exist it is important to determine their relationship with the respective classes and to assess the degree in which the parties express the interests of the various classes.

8. Which parties are in power? What is their relationship to the respective classes? Who controls the military order, the police, or their functional equivalents?

9. What patterns, regularities or trends can be observed in the changes within and among the classes? Which classes are growing numerically? Which are diminishing? Which functions are becoming more important? Which less important? For example, in the case of automation it was seen that the role of unskilled workers is diminishing in production.

10. What is the relationship among the major institutional orders of society, e.g., the economic, political, military, legal, religious, etc.? Which of these determine the tempo and direction of change in the society? Where are the key decisions made for the society as a whole? What is the relationship between the "power elite" and the economically dominant classes?

11. How do the external relations of a society affect its development? Such problems as international relations should not be overlooked. Marx never treated a society as a closed system.

12. Locate the radical elements in the society, i.e., those classes putting forward the most radical demands for change and having an objective interest in change. What are their explicit political aims as expressed directly by them or by their political representatives? Conversely, which classes have most interest in preserving the *status quo?*

13. What representation or power do the subordinate classes have in the government? What is the political program of each party, i.e., what are its declared political aims? Contrast this with actual policies and actions.

14. Are there any coalitions, economic or political, among the classes and parties? What trends can be observed in these coalitions? Which are the conservative and which the radical elements?

15. What is the role of the "great man," or charismatic leader,

in the society? For example, what Marx attempted in his *18th Brumaire* was to "demonstrate how the *class struggle* in France created circumstances and relationships that made it possible for a mediocrity to play a hero's part." [45]

16. What are some of the central ideological themes of the society? Whose interests do these themes tend to serve?

17. Consider the historical context of the society in question. For example, in studying American society in the 20th century, *generalizations* based on the period from 1914 to 1946, which included two world-wars, an economic crisis and a prolonged depression, would be quite different from those based on the period of 1946 to 1966, which included none of these.

18. The role of tradition should not be ignored. Does a revolutionary, militaristic, or any other kind of tradition prevail? "Men make their own history," said Marx, "but they do not make it just as they please; they do not make it under circumstances chosen by themselves, but under circumstances directly encountered, given and transmitted from the past. The tradition of all the dead generations weighs like a nightmare on the brain of the living." [46]

19. Consider the size and role of the state bureaucracy. Which of its administrative functions are necessary for the society as a whole? Which functions directly benefit only certain classes?

20. What is the role of the legislative body of the government? Is it an effective body or afflicted with what Marx called *parliamentary cretinism*? Is its legislation, designed to improve the conditions of the subordinate classes, enforced?

This list is intended to be merely suggestive and is far from exhaustive. It points to the various factors which Marx considered in his more concrete studies of society. This paradigm together with the general premises of his theoretical approach are what make Marx's work relevant to contemporary social-science inquiry.

NOTES

1. Marx and Engels, *Selected Correspondence*. Moscow: Foreign Languages Publishing House, 1953, p. 412.

2. Engels' letters, Part 3, Ref. 8, on p. 116 of this book, in which he speaks of economic necessity asserting itself "ultimately," "in the final analysis," etc.

3. Engels, *op. cit.*, p. 504.

4. *Ibid.*, p. 504.

5. *Ibid.*, p. 505.

6. *Ibid.*, p. 505.

7. *Ibid.*, pp. 505-506.

8. *Ibid.*, p. 496.

9. Karl Marx, *A Contribution to the Critique of Political Economy*. Chicago: Charles H. Kerr and Company, 1904, p. 11.

10. No thought is an orphan. Surely one can find this idea, at least in its implicit form, among many of Marx's antecedents, notably Montesquieu. Credit, however, may be given to Marx for the explicitness with which he developed the idea.

11. *Ibid.*, p. 12.

12. *Ibid.*, p. 12.

13. Karl Marx and Frederick Engels, *The German Ideology*. New York: International Publishers, 1960, p. 14.

14. *German Ideology,* quoted in T. B. Bottomore and Maximilien Rubel, *Karl Marx: Selected Writings in Sociology and Social Philosophy*. London: Watts and Co., 1961, p. 78.

15. See the fascinating discussion of this problem in Marx and Engels, *op. cit.*, pp. 39-43.

16. F. Engels, Introduction to *The Class Struggles in France,* MESW I, p. 109.

17. Marx, *The Class Struggles in France,* MESW I, pp. 128-129. In this section, references will hereafter be designated by the page number in parentheses following the quoted passage.

18. Engels, *Selected Correspondence, op. cit.*, p. 507.

19. Engels, MESW I, p. 110.

20. *Ibid.*, p. 110.

21. *Ibid.*, p. 110.

22. *Ibid.*, p. 111.

23. *Ibid.*, p. 115.

24. This work was written mainly by Engels. For a long time it was believed that Marx was the author but the correspondence between them reveals that although the *New York Daily Tribune* had proposed the work to Marx, it was Engels who in the main carried it out with Marx collaborating. In discussing this work, I therefore use Engels' name but attribute the ideas to both thinkers.

25. Karl Marx, *Selected Works* Vol. II. International Publishers, N.D., p. 40.

26. Marx, *op. cit.*, p. 41.

27. Joseph Schumpeter, "The Decade of the Twenties," *American Economic Review Supplement,* 36 (1946), pp. 1-10, quoted by Seymour Martin Lipset, *Political Man.* New York: Anchor Books, Doubleday & Co. Inc., 1963, p. 287.

28. Engels, *op. cit.*, p. 42.

29. *Ibid.*, p. 43.
30. *Ibid.*, p. 43.
31. *Ibid.*, p. 44.
32. *Ibid.*, p. 46.
33. *Ibid.*, p. 47.
34. *Ibid.*, p. 47.
35. *Ibid.*, p. 146.
36. Although this work cannot be properly classified with Marx's journalistic writings, it is considered here because it also deals with the revolutionary events of the time.
37. Engels, MESW I, p. 430.
38. *Ibid.*, p. 432.
39. *Ibid.*, p. 433.
40. *Ibid.*, p. 435.
41. *Ibid.*, p. 435.
42. *Ibid.*, p. 438.
43. *Ibid.*, p. 438.
44. *Ibid.*, p. 439.
45. MESW I, p. 222.
46. *Ibid.*, p. 225.

Conclusion

THE STUDY HAS ATTEMPTED TO SHOW THAT MARX'S WORK TAKEN as a whole is invaluable for an understanding of whole societies in the process of historical change. This was recognized at the end of the 19th century and from that time it became increasingly relevant to the social sciences as they were being developed in the universities. There was hardly a famous social thinker of the late 19th and early 20th century who did not in some way take Marx's work into account, explicitly accepting, modifying or rejecting it. Perhaps the most conspicuous case of a critical and partial adoption of Marx's method is the work of Max Weber.

Weber, who has been called the "bourgeois Marx," was an admirer of Marx's historical method and its underlying hypothesis. He did not regard his own studies of the Protestant influence on the origin and development of capitalism as a final or dogmatic formulation of the problem. Nor did he regard these studies as a refutation of Marx, as some of the interpretations of his work have suggested. Weber intended his work as a preliminary investigation of the influence of certain religious ideas on the development of the central values or spirit of capitalism as an economic system. This is clear from his own account of his intentions:

> Here we have only attempted to trace the fact and the direction of its [Protestantism's] influence to their motives in one, though a very important point. But it would also further be necessary to investigate how protestant Asceticism was in turn influenced in its development and its character by the totality of social conditions, especially economic . . . . But it is, of course, not my aim to substitute for a one-sided materialistic an equally one-sided spiritualistic causal interpretation of culture and of history. Each is equally possible, but each, if it does not serve as the preparation, but as the conclusion of an investigation, accomplishes equally little in the interest of historical truth.[1]

159

Weber, then, did not seek a psychological determination of economic events, but emphasized the fundamental importance of the economic factor. As Ephraim Fischoff has pointed out, Weber "recognized that capitalism would have arisen without Protestantism, in fact that it had done so in many culture complexes; and that it would not and did not come about where the objective conditions were not ripe for it." [2]

We have seen from Marx's treatment of the events of his time that he took a variety of factors into consideration, notably the political, and made no attempt to reconstruct events to fit an *a priori* conception. In the journalistic writings, his method is revealed not so much as an effort to impute causal priority to the economic order as an effort to determine precisely the relationship between the economic and the other orders of society. This being the case, he probably would have been amenable to Weber's "generalization" of his method. In a sense, a large part of Weber's debate with the ghost of Marx was carried on by taking over the latter's method and applying it with great skill and refinement. This is precisely what he proposed to do when he assumed the editorship of the *Archiv fur Sozialwissenschaft und Sozialpolitik,* and used Marx's method strictly as a heuristic principle. In doing so he was actually debating not Marx but the Marxists. For it was in fact not Marx but the latter who turned the so-called materialistic conception into a monistic interpretation of history.

What did Weber attempt to do with Marx's method? In what way did he refine it? A large part of Weber's work can be viewed as an attempt to "round-out" Marx's "economic determinism" with a political and military determinism. If Marx related social classes and political factors in each economic period to control over the means of production, Weber sought to explain political power by disposition over weapons and over means of administration. For Weber, "Attention to the control of the material means of political power is as crucial for grasping the types of political structure as is attention to the means of production in the case of Marx for grasping economic structures." [3] That Marx would have viewed this approach as harmonious with his own seems to be a justifiable inference from his concrete analyses in which he did in fact give the required attention to political and military factors. In no sense did he attempt in his journalistic writings to explain everything in terms of the sphere of production or even the total economic order. On the other hand, the fact that Marx did not give the non-economic factors the prominence they deserve in his purely theoretical formulations, caused serious distortions of his method after him. This led to vulgar Marxism among his self-appointed disciples and Weber was therefore right in criticizing the latter for not carefully distinguishing the "strictly economic" from the "economically determined" and these, in turn, from the "economically relevant."

Weber also shared the view that ideological phenomena were correlated with the "material" interests of the economic and political orders. If Marx's work implied a functional determination of the former by the latter, Weber posited instead the principle of "elective affinity," but nevertheless viewed the ideological spheres as not strictly autonomous in their development. Weber, like Marx, attempted to grasp the interrelations of all institutional orders making up a social structure. What Weber's reinterpretation of Marx's view shows is that the insight which Marx gained by his economic emphasis could be generalized and, consequently, made more fruitful. A good example of this is Weber's generalization of Marx's emphasis on the wage worker being "separated" from the means of production. To this Weber replied that the modern soldier is also "separated" from the means of violence, the scientist from the means of research, and the civil and business official from the means of administration. He thus placed Marx's approach in a more general context and showed that "Marx's conclusions rest upon observations drawn from a dramatized 'special case,' which is better seen as one case in a broad series of similar cases." [4] It is this kind of imaginative utilization of Marx's ideas which is necessary if they are to fructify social and political research.

The value of Marx's method for the study of whole societies in the process of change is clear. It calls attention to the most essential general trends shared by societies of a certain type along with the differences they manifest according to time and place. This is precisely what Marx had in mind when he constructed a general model of capitalist society but recognized that differences among capitalist societies must be explained by their historically specific conditions. The student who would grasp the structure and mechanics of change of whole societies would do well to consider Marx's method, at least as a point of departure. In doing so the important thing to keep in mind is that Marx's erroneous assumptions about the political and other developments in the West do not necessarily affect that which is really important about his work, namely, his general approach. Many of Marx's ideas have been incorporated into present-day social science and have become its permanent acquisition. And this incorporation, which has made a "Marxian" social science superfluous, leaves little doubt that nondogmatic Marxism will continue to provide insights into the workings of social systems, and enlighten social research generally.

NOTES

1. Max Weber, *The Protestant Ethic and the Spirit of Capitalism*. Translated by Talcott Parsons. New York: Charles Scribner's Sons, 1958, p. 183.

2. Ephraim Fischoff, "The History of a Controversy," in *Protestantism and Capitalism*. Edited by Robert W. Green. Boston: D. C. Heath and Company, 1959, pp. 109-110.

3. H. H. Gerth and C. Wright Mills, *From Max Weber: Essays in Sociology*. New York: Oxford University Press, 1958, p. 47.

4. *Ibid.*, p. 50.

Bibliography

Books

Adams, H. P. *Karl Marx in His Earlier Writings*. London: George Allen and Unwin Ltd., 1940.

Black, Max (ed.). *The Social Theories of Talcott Parsons*. Englewood Cliffs, New Jersey: Prentice-Hall, 1961.

Bober, M. M. *Karl Marx's Interpretation of History*. Cambridge: Harvard University Press, 1950.

Bottomore, T. B., and Rubel, Maximilien. *Karl Marx: Selected Writings in Sociology and Social Philosophy*. London: Watts & Co., 1961.

Burdick, Eugene, and Brodbeck, Arthur J. *American Voting Behavior*. Glencoe, Illinois: The Free Press, 1959.

Butler, E. M. *The Saint Simonian Religion in Germany*. Cambridge: Harvard University Press, 1926.

Calvez, Jean-Yves. *La Pensée de Karl Marx*. Paris: Editions Du Seuil, 1956.

Chang, Sherman H. M. *The Marxian Theory of the State*. Philadelphia: John Spencer, Inc., 1931.

Dahrendorf, Ralf. *Class and Class Conflict in Industrial Society*. Stanford, California: Stanford University Press, 1959.

Dreher, Carl. *Automation*. New York: W. W. Norton & Co., Inc., 1957.

Durkheim, Emile. *Socialism*. Edited by Alvin W. Gouldner. New York: Collier Books, 1962.

Eastman, Max. *Marxism: Is It Science?* New York: W. W. Norton & Co., Inc., 1940.

Engels, Frederick. *Anti-Duhring*. Moscow: Foreign Languages Publishing House, 1954.

Engels, Frederick. *Germany: Revolution and Counterrevolution. Selected Works* Vol. II. New York: International Publishers, N. D.

Fromm, Erich. *Marx's Concept of Man*. New York: Frederick Ungar Publishing Co., 1961.

Gerth, H. H., and Mills, C. Wright. *From Max Weber: Essays in Sociology*. New York: Oxford University Press, 1958.

Green, Robert W. (ed.). *Protestantism and Capitalism: The Weber Thesis and Its Critics*. Boston: D. C. Heath & Co., 1959.

163

Korsch, Karl. *Karl Marx*. London: Chapman & Hall Ltd., 1938.

Lipset, Seymour Martin. *Political Man*. Garden City, New York: Anchor Books, 1963.

MacIver, Robert M. *The Web of Government*. New York: Macmillan, 1947.

Marcuse, Herbert. *Reason and Revolution*. Boston: Beacon Press, 1960.

Marx, Karl. *Capital* Vol. I. Moscow: Foreign Languages Publishing House, 1954.

Marx, Karl. *Capital* Vol. II. Moscow: Foreign Languages Publishing House, 1962.

Marx, Karl. *Capital* Vol. III. Moscow: Foreign Languages Publishing House, 1962.

Marx, Karl, and Engels, Frederick. *The Civil War in France* cited from *Karl Marx and Frederick Engels Selected Works* (2 vols.). Moscow: Foreign Language Publishing House, 1950.

Marx, Karl, and Engels, Frederick. *The Class Struggles in France* cited from *Karl Marx and Frederick Engels Selected Works* (2 vols.). Moscow: Foreign Language Publishing House, 1950.

Marx, Karl, and Engels, Frederick. *Communist Manifesto*. London: George Allen & Unwin Ltd., 1948.

Marx, Karl. *A Contribution to the Critique of Political Economy*. Chicago: Charles H. Kerr & Co., 1904.

Marx, Karl. *Economic and Philosophic Manuscripts of 1844*. Moscow: Foreign Languages Publishing House, 1961.

Marx, Karl, and Engels, Frederick. *The Eighteenth Brumaire of Louis Bonaparte* cited from *Karl Marx and Frederick Engels Selected Works* (2 vols.). Moscow: Foreign Language Publishing House, 1950.

Marx, Karl, and Engels, Frederick. *The German Ideology*. New York: International Publishers, 1960.

Marx, Karl. *Germany: Revolution and Counter-Revolution* cited from *Karl Marx Selected Works* (2 vols.). New York: International Publishers, N. D.

Marx, Karl. *The Poverty of Philosophy*. Moscow: Foreign Languages Publishing House, N. D.

Marx, Karl, and Engels, Frederick. *Selected Correspondence*. Moscow: Foreign Languages Publishing House, 1953.

Marx, Karl, and Engels, Frederick. *Werke Band 13*. Berlin: Dietz Verlag, 1961.

Mayer, Gustav. *Friedrich Engels*. New York: Alfred A. Knopf, 1936.

Mehring, Franz. *Karl Marx*. Ann Arbor: University of Michigan Press, 1962.

Mills, C. Wright. *The Marxists*. New York: Dell Publishing Co., 1962.

Mills, C. Wright. *White Collar*. New York: Oxford University Press, 1956.

Model, Roland and Stone. *The Scientific-Industrial Revolution*. New York: Twentieth Century Press, 1957.

Moore, Wilbert E. *Industrialization and Labor: Social Aspects of Economic Development*. Ithaca and New York: Cornell University Press, 1951.

Moore, Wilbert E. *Social Change*. Englewood Cliffs, New Jersey: Prentice-Hall, Inc., 1963.

Nicolaievsky, B., and Maenchen-Helgen, O. *Karl Marx: Man and Fighter*. Philadelphia and London: J. B. Lippincott Co., 1936.

Perlman, Selig. *A Theory of the Labor Movement*. New York: Augustus M. Kelly, 1949.

Russell, Bertrand. *A History of Western Philosophy*. New York: Simon and Schuster, 1963.

Schumpeter, Joseph A. *Capitalism, Socialism and Democracy*. New York: Harper & Row Publishers, Inc., 1962.

Sweezy, Paul M. *The Theory of Capitalist Development*. New York: Monthly Review Press, 1956.

Tawney, R. H. *Religion and the Rise of Capitalism*. New York: Harcourt, Brace & Co., 1926.

Taylor, Frederick W. *Scientific Management*. New York and London: Harper, 1947.

Tillich, Paul. *Der Mensch im Christentum und im Marxismus*. Dusseldorf: 1953.

Tucker, Robert C. *Philosophy and Myth in Karl Marx*. Cambridge: Harvard University Press, 1961.

Weber, Max. *General Economic History*. New York: Collier Books, 1961.

Weber, Max. *The Protestant Ethic and the Spirit of Capitalism*. New York: Charles Scribner's Sons, 1958.

Weiss, John. *Moses Hess Utopian Socialist*. Detroit: Wayne State University Press, 1960.

Articles and Documents

Bell, Daniel. "The Debate on Alienation," *Revisionism: Essays on the History of Marxist Ideas*. Edited by Leopold Labedz. New York: Frederick A. Praeger, 1962.

Buckingham, Walter S. *Hearings Before the Subcommittee on Economic Stabilization*. 84th Congress, Washington, D. C., October, 1955.

Feuer, Lewis S. "A Symposium on C. Wright Mills' 'The Sociological Imagination,'" *Berkeley Journal of Sociology* (Berkeley: University of California, Dept. of Sociology, Fall 1959), Vol. V, No. I, pp. 122-123.

Feuer, Lewis. "What Is Alienation? The Career of a Concept," in *Sociology on Trial*. Edited by Maurice Stein & Arthur Vidich. Englewood Cliffs, New Jersey: Prentice-Hall, Inc., 1963.

Final Report of the Select Committee on Small Business, House of Representatives, 87th Congress, House Report No. 2569, Washington: 1963.

Fischoff, Ephraim. "The History of a Controversy," in *Protestantism and Capitalism: The Weber Thesis and Its Critics.* Edited by Robert W. Green. Boston: D. C. Heath & Co., 1959.

Hacker, Andrew. "Towards a Corporate America," 59th Annual Conference of the American Political Science Association, September, 1963. Also in *New York Times,* Saturday, September 7, 1963.

Lichtheim, George. "Marx and His Critics," *Problems of Communism* Vol. XI, No. 4, July-Aug., 1962.

Schumpeter, Joseph. "The Decade of the Twenties," *American Economic Review Supplement,* 36 (1946), pp. 1-10.

Seligman, Ben. "Man, Work and the Automated Feast," *Commentary,* July, 1962.

Index